ONE TO THE WOLVES

ONE TO THE
WOLVES

A DESPERATE MOTHER ON THE TRAIL OF A KILLER

Lois Duncan

This edition published in 2015 by:

Planet Ann Rule, LLC

Seattle, WA

ISBN 10: 1-940018-51-X

ISBN 13: 978-1-940018-51-5

CONTENTS

for "Kait's Army"
with gratitude

This is a true story. The facts are documented. Several names have been changed to protect individuals who might be endangered if they were identified.

Excerpts from newspaper articles are used with permission of *The Albuquerque Journal, The Albuquerque Tribune, The L.A. Times,* and *The John Cooke Fraud Report* and are copyrighted in the names of those publications.

Psychic readings that pertain to particular events that are described in the text but are not paramount to the story are numbered as footnotes and presented in full in the Appendix.

"The only thing necessary for the triumph of
evil is for good men to do nothing."
—*Edmund Burke* (1729–1797)

FOREWORD BY ANN RULE

When it comes to researching true crime, the hardest part for me has always been meeting the families of victims. I *want* to meet them, of course, so they can tell me about the sons and daughters, fathers and mothers, and brothers and sisters who were taken from them so cruelly.

It is my job to give the victim a voice, and I've sat at more kitchen tables than I can count as mothers shuffle through boxes of old photos and tell me stories of the long gone children who once brightened their lives.

We cry—and sometimes laugh—together, as they remember out loud both the bad times and good. As their families tell me about them, the victims come alive in my mind. When I see the agony in the mothers' eyes, I feel just a hint of their pain, but that is necessary if I am to paint an accurate picture.

I often find myself humbled by the strength of mothers who fight their way through a grief that I can't begin to imagine.

In many cases, the mothers have yet to get justice for their murdered children. Ronda Reynold's case comes to mind. In my book, *In the Still of The Night,* I wrote about Ronda's mother, Barbara Thompson, and her crusade for justice for her daughter. In 1998, Ronda was a former Washington State Trooper, living in Toledo, Washington, with her new husband of less than a year and three stepsons.

She was found shot to death in a closet in her home, twelve feet from where her husband slept. He claimed he did not wake—did not hear the deafening blast of the gun. Detectives took his statement at face value, and Ronda's death was ruled a suicide.

But Barbara knew her daughter did not take her own life, and she doggedly investigated, sometimes putting herself in danger. As of this writing, no one has been convicted of Ronda's murder, but because of her mother's persistence, there was a small victory in 2011. A coroner's jury returned a unanimous verdict of homicide, and the coroner changed Ronda's death certificate to reflect that.

And then there is Eleanore Rose. Her eighteen-year-old daughter, Denise Naslund, was abducted and killed by Ted Bundy in July 1974. He snatched her and Janice Ott from Lake Sammamish State Park on a sizzling day with thousands of people cramming the beach.

Overwhelmed by grief, Eleanore Rose wore black for the rest of her life. Though crushed by her loss, she sought justice for Denise and other murder victims.

Eleanore was appalled when the death penalty in Washington State was abolished in 1975, and she campaigned relentlessly to bring it back. She went door to door, a frail figure in a black dress, and told her story to anyone who would listen. Most people were sympathetic to the grieving mother. Eleanore collected a fat stack of signed petitions, and contributed to the 1978 reinstatement of capital punishment.

Bundy did not face the gallows in Washington, but died in the electric chair at Raiford Prison in Starke, Florida, in January 1989. If Bundy had returned to Washington, the death penalty was waiting for him here. Eleanore Rose had seen to that.

Mothers seeking justice for their murdered children are not a rarity. Lois Duncan will tell you that there are far too many. She has received hundreds of letters from them, some with the ink smeared by tears. She dearly wishes that she could not empathize with them. She would give anything to not be able to understand how they feel.

But Lois does know how they feel.

She joined their ranks a lifetime ago when her youngest child was murdered.

When I met Lois Duncan in the mid 1960s, I never dreamed that I would one day be her friend—that I would be sitting here now, writing the foreword for this book.

When I first met Lois, I did not actually *meet* her, but watched in awe from the audience as she gave a presentation at The Pacific Northwest Writer's Conference in Tacoma, Washington. I was an aspiring writer, but Lois was published, and she was there to tell the rest of us how we could become published, too.

She and I would cross paths again, many years later, and we noted similarities in our journeys as writers. We both know what it is like to be a divorced mother with many mouths to feed. And we both started out writing for the pulps—the cheaper magazines with the pulpy pages—before graduating to the "slicks. " We even wrote for some of the same publications, including *Woman's Day, Ladies Home Journal,* and *Good Housekeeping.*

Yes, we had similarities, but differences, too.

Lois had always known she would become an author, but I had no such wish. When I was a little girl, I thought, "One thing I would never want to do is write a book, because it would be too much work!"

Lois was ten when she began submitting articles, and she was only thirteen when she was first published.

I didn't want to be an author. I wanted to be a police officer. Growing up, I had spent my summers in jail! My grandfather was the Sheriff in Stanton, Michigan. He and my grandmother ran a "ma and pa jail." My grandmother cooked the meals for the prisoners, and I delivered the trays of food to them.

A murderess taught me how to knit and to "never trust women who pluck their eyebrows into itty bitty lines."

Both my grandfather and an uncle were sheriffs, my cousin was a prosecuting attorney, and another uncle was a medical examiner. I guess the taste for crime fighting is in my blood, and I could not wait to grow up and work in law enforcement.

But when I went to college—Willamette University and University of Washington—I discovered that writing classes were an easy "A" for me, and I ended up taking so many of them that I earned a BA in creative writing with minors in psychology, criminology and penology.

At 22, I realized my dream and became a Seattle policewoman. My beat was the Pioneer Square area in downtown Seattle. Female officers wore skirts and high heels and were not allowed to carry guns. Still, I was thrilled.

But it did not last long, because I failed the eye test. Without my glasses I was legally blind. If I were to lose my glasses in a struggle, I would be helpless to defend myself. My career in law enforcement was over.

I was so heartbroken that I could not bear to drive by the Seattle Police Department for many years. The one thing that fascinated me more than any other was out of my reach.

I married and had four children. Meanwhile, Lois had done the same.

Lois's first marriage ended, and she wrote like the wind, her fingers flying over the keys on her old fashioned typewriter as she churned out articles to support her family. My marriage, too, would end, but when I went to the Pacific Northwest Writers' conference, I was a housewife and Brownie leader, hoping to learn how to sell articles to supplement our family's income while my husband went back to school to earn his teaching degree.

When I attended the conference, I was so shy that I barely spoke to anyone. But I was excited to be breathing the same air as real writers. I sat in my hotel room alone that night, unaware that all attendees were invited to a party where they could mingle with the authors, editors and agents.

The highlight of the conference for me was hearing Lois Duncan's talk about writing for the confession magazines—glossy covered pulps that had been around for decades. True confessions, Lois explained, weren't really true, but the writers had to sign contracts stating that the stories were based on something that had actually happened to someone somewhere. They paid about three cents a word, but Lois said that a fast writer could make ends meet writing for the genre.

Inspired by Lois Duncan, I went home and started confessing. I sold about two dozen confession stories, and then, with my new found confidence, I moved onto the detective magazines. Unlike the confession magazines, the detective magazines were factual, and it was essential that the reporters understood police procedure and forensics.

So I took classes such as "crime scene investigation" and "arrest, search and seizure," eventually earning another degree. I would write over a thousand detective stories over the next decade. I was in my element, welcomed back into the bosom of the Seattle Police Department where they gave me access to their files.

Meanwhile, Lois Duncan's career was thriving. She wrote a number of bestselling young adult suspense novels and children's books. Some of her books have been made into movies, including, the major motion pictures *Hotel For Dogs* and *I Know What You Did Last Summer*.

But Lois was living in Albuquerque, and I was in Seattle, and it would be many years before we were once again both at the same writers' conference at the same time.

When my daughter, Leslie, told me about her favorite author, Lois Duncan, I did not make the connection. I did not realize that the author Leslie was so enthralled with was the very author who had inspired me to start *my* career as a writer all those years ago.

By the time Lois and I did meet again, both she and I had written a number of bestsellers. Our genres had been very different over the last few years. I was writing true crime, and she was writing for teens and children.

But now, I was horrified to learn, Lois had switched to true crime because tragedy had struck her family. She was writing a book about the murder of her very own daughter. I read Lois's *Who Killed My Daughter?* and provided a cover blurb.

I was impressed with Lois, both as an author and a friend. She was fun and interesting, and she and her husband Don Arquette, and their daughter, Robin, flew to Seattle to stay a few days with me and Leslie in my beach house. We all had a great time and felt like we had known each other forever.

Though Lois was at the top of the heap of authors in the YA genre, she set aside that lucrative career to focus on one thing:

justice for Kait.

Kaitlyn Arquette, 18, was killed in a drive by shooting in Albuquerque in July 1989. No one has been tried, let alone convicted for her murder.

Police figured it was a random shooting, but as Lois investigated, she discovered that her daughter had been targeted. The wonderful, smart young woman who planned to become a doctor had been drawn into an illegal scheme. In too deep, Kait tried to free herself, but she knew secrets that others feared she would tell. It cost her her life.

But proving this was a difficult and dangerous task. As diligently as a detective, Lois followed a trail that wound and twisted and became so treacherous at times that her family had to flee when their lives were threatened.

Lois chronicled the astounding tale in her book, *Who Killed My Daughter?*

It was a huge success and received rave reviews, but it did not accomplish the one thing Lois had hoped for. The book did bring witnesses out of the woodwork, and they offered bits and pieces of information that propelled Lois forward, but as of yet, there has been no justice for Kaitlyn Arquette.

A quarter of a century has passed since Kait's murder, and if she had not been killed, Kait would now be 43. She likely would have realized her dream of becoming a doctor, and by now she probably would have married and had children—maybe even *grandchildren*.

Lois marks each passing year, each month, each *day*, thinking about the life Kait would have lived if she had not been so cruelly taken from this earth.

Like Barbara Thompson, Eleanore Rose, and thousands of other

LOIS DUNCAN

mothers of murdered children, Lois knows that life goes on. But for them, time stands still. When Lois closes her eyes and pictures Kait, she sees a smiling a teenager stuck in 1989.

Lois will not give up until Kait's murder is solved. And, so, she has written another book. *One to the Wolves* is not a sequel to *Who Killed My Daughter?* but a stand alone book with its own revelations, expertly crafted by one of America's most talented authors.

I suspect that you will be as mesmerized by it as I was.

—Ann Rule *(2014)*

Lois Duncan with friend, true crime author Ann Rule, around 1992.

(Author's collection)

PREFACE

Albuquerque Tribune, July 18, 1989

BRIGHT FUTURE OF SHINING TEEN DIES IN GUNSHOTS

by Lynn Bartels, staff reporter

Kaitlyn Arquette, a recent graduate of Highland High School, was shot in the head Sunday night as she drove home after having dinner with a girlfriend. The 18-year-old student, whose mother writes critically acclaimed teen books under the name of Lois Duncan, died Monday night at University Hospital. Police have no leads in the shooting.

Arquette appeared to have been driving east on Lomas Boulevard with her windows up when she was shot. She then crashed into a light pole at 401 Lomas Blvd. N.E.

"Kait was a straight arrow," said Arquette's sister, 32-year-old Kerry Mahrer of Dallas. "She worked fulltime at an import store throughout her senior year of high school and still held down shining grades."

Mahrer said her sister planned to be a physician and was taking summer classes at the University of New Mexico.

Mahrer said her parents, Don and Lois Arquette, "were doing as well as could be expected—lousy."

Other survivors include a sister, Robin, 34, of Florida, and brothers, Brett, 31, and Don Jr., 21, of Albuquerque.

Albuquerque Journal, July 21, 1989

GRAY VW SOUGHT IN KILLING; MEMORIAL SERVICE HELD FOR VICTIM

by Glen Rosales, staff writer

Albuquerque police are searching for a gray Volkswagen they say may be connected to the shooting of Kaitlyn Arquette... "We are not saying this is a suspect's car," police Chief Sam Baca said during a news conference. "It was seen around the area around the time of the shooting."

Outside the funeral, Kaitlyn's girlfriends filed past Dung Nguyen, Kaitlyn's boyfriend, hugging and consoling him.

Later, he talked about the night Kaitlyn was shot.

"I waited and waited for her," Nguyen said. "But she never came home. Nobody called me. Nobody told me nothing. Then police came to the door. They started searching my house, going through everything. They asked my whereabouts that night. They asked if I had a gun. I kept asking them, 'What happened?' When they told me, I went down there, but she had already been taken to the hospital. I went to the hospital. It didn't look like her. I didn't know who she was."

LOIS DUNCAN

Albuquerque Tribune, January 18, 1990

THREE ARRESTED IN SLAYING OF ARQUETTE

by Cary Tyler, staff reporter

Three men have been arrested in the shooting death of Kaitlyn Arquette.

Juvenal Escobedo, 21; Miguel Garcia, 18; and Dennis "Marty" Martinez, 18, were arrested Wednesday night. The suspects were charged on open counts of murder and using a gun in a crime. They are being held at the City-County Jail. A Crime Stopper's tip led to the arrests, Herrera said.

Arquette was the youngest of five children and daughter of author Lois Arquette, who uses the pen name, Lois Duncan. Her father, Donald, is an electrical engineer at Sandia National Laboratories.

Arquette's heart and lungs were donated to a Santa Fe man at Presbyterian Hospital who received a rare lung-heart transplant. Her liver was donated to a man in the Los Angeles area, her kidneys went to a San Francisco patient, and her pancreas was sent to Miami for research.

Before the shooting, Arquette had dinner with a friend. Arquette was invited to spend the night with her friend, but declined, saying she had to study for a summer school class.

XXIV

Albuquerque Journal, February 10, 1990

TEEN SAYS HE LIED TO POLICE ABOUT
SEEING ARQUETTE SHOOTING

by Sonny Lopez and Steve Shoup

Robert Garcia admits he lied to Albuquerque police when he told them he witnessed the shooting of Kaitlyn Arquette during a joy ride with three friends, but he says police pressured him to tell the story...

Garcia, 16, said he was interviewed by police for more than nine hours. He said he initially told officers the truth–that he was in the Youth Diagnostic and Development Center the night Arquette was killed–but then changed his story. He says he lied to satisfy investigators, who he claims threatened him with arrest and prison.

"They started scaring me and stuff," Garcia said.

He also said the men who were arrested had never told him they had been involved in the shooting death.

LOIS DUNCAN

Albuquerque Journal, March 1, 1990

ARQUETTE SLAYING SUSPECT MISSING; WARRANT ISSUED

by Susanne Burks and Lea Lorber

A man indicted in connection with the killing of Kaitlyn Arquette did not turn himself in to his attorney Wednesday, and despite a bench warrant for his arrest was not in custody late Wednesday night. . . .

Assistant Public Defender Lorenzo Chacon, who represents Juvenal Escobedo, said. . . "I can only speculate he's been frightened off by all the commotion."

Escobedo and Miguel Juan Garcia were indicted late Tuesday on charges of first-degree murder and related crimes. Garcia remains in the city-county jail in lieu of bond in an unrelated burglary-larceny case.

A spokeswoman for the Albuquerque Police Department said that no all-points bulletin had been issued for Escobedo. She said she didn't know whether police attempted to arrest Escobedo and she knew nothing else about the case.

Chacon said he talked to members of Escobedo's family Wednesday and "they were under the impression he turned himself in. His girlfriend thought police had picked him up last night."

XXVI

Albuquerque Journal, July 8, 1990

KAITLYN ARQUETTE'S DEATH SNARLED IN CONTRADICTIONS

by Mike Gallagher, Investigative Reporter

The Kaitlyn Arquette slaying was described by police as a random shooting: a few drunken young men in a car firing a pistol on a dare.

But police reports indicate the case against the two men now charged with the shooting might be shaky. The reports show witnesses who have given contradictory information, statements since recanted, and little in the way of physical evidence. The reports also disclose other theories have been offered about Arquette's killing. . .

It was a shooting that shocked the city, and once police had leads in the case they used nearly every possible tactic to solve it.

Homicide investigators hypnotized a witness, hid a tape recorder in a jail holding cell, used a lie detector test, relied on Crime Stoppers tips and used interrogation techniques that will be challenged in court.

There was little apparent progress in the case for six months–until a Crime Stoppers tipster identified four suspects as the killers.

On Jan. 17, 1990, detectives arrested the four. Two of the suspects gave police statements identifying Juvenal Escobedo and Miguel Garcia as the two mainly responsible for the shooting. Robert Garcia, who is no relation to Miguel, told police he watched Miguel Garcia fire three shots from a .22-caliber revolver at a car. Police obtained a similar statement from Dennis "Marty" Martinez.

Police had to back off Garcia's statement when they learned he was in the Youth Diagnostic Center the night of the killing. Martinez has since recanted. Garcia remains in jail, but Escobedo is a fugitive.

Police reports don't reveal any independent eyewitnesses to the shooting and no scientific evidence linking Garcia and Escobedo to the killing.

The reports also show detectives didn't consider Arquette's live-in boyfriend, Dung Ngoc Nguyen, to be a suspect. Reports do show police were told the couple's relationship was stormy, with Arquette having threatened to throw him out of the apartment, and one person told officers that Nguyen had involved her in an alleged insurance fraud.

Albuquerque Journal, July 8, 1990

POLICE CLEAR BOYFRIEND, BUT RUMORS PERSIST

by Mike Gallagher, investigative reporter

On Feb. 3, 1990, on orders of the District Attorney's Office to clean up any loose ends in the Kaitlyn Arquette murder case, city police re-inter-viewed Arquette's Vietnamese boyfriend, Dung Ngoc Nguyen. Nguyen, 26, had never been a suspect in the homicide as far as detectives were concerned, although Arquette's girlfriends told police the relationship was marked by bitter arguments.

Within a week of her July 1989 murder, Nguyen attempted to commit suicide. Nguyen told detectives he was depressed over Ar-quette's death and thought everyone blamed him. . . . Their apartment manager told police shortly after Arquette's death that the couple ar-gued frequently and that she once came to his apartment late at night because she was afraid. Arquette also told the manager she was going to force Nguyen to move out.

Police reports show that Arquette's friends also told detectives she had participated in insurance fraud with Nguyen in a staged car acci-dent during a trip to California. There were three unexplained telephone calls made to California from Arquette's apartment the day after she was shot and Nguyen, witnesses said, was at the hospital with her family.

Reports show detectives didn't follow up on the information until after the arrests of Miguel Garcia and Juvenal Escobedo. In the February interview with police, Nguyen denied any involvement in an insurance scam. He denied that Arquette was going to kick him out of the apartment or that he was a member of a Vietnamese gang.

But police reports indicate Nguyen's friends had a different story. Ray Padilla was with Nguyen when he first met Kaitlyn Arquette about a year before her death. It was Padilla who talked to police about the alleged California insurance scam. Padilla told police Arquette didn't use drugs, but Nguyen's friends in California were cocaine dealers.

Albuquerque Journal, April 24, 1991

DA DROPS CHARGES IN ARQUETTE SHOOTING

by Suzanne Burks and Mike Gallagher

Miguel Juan Garcia, 19, walked out of the Bernalillo County Deten-tion Center at about four P.M. (today), after fifteen months in jail. Carrying a Bible and a garbage bag full of his belongings, Garcia said he felt "blessed" to be free. . .

District Attorney Bob Schwartz said he dropped the charges be-cause "there's been some erosion in the state's case . . . and then there seemed to be this other angle while the state's case was dwindling."

He said the new angle was "the emergence of these other facts re-garding her association with this group of Vietnamese."

He said he informed police homicide Sgt. Ruth Lowe Tuesday that he was dropping the charges and that Lowe said "they would be very interested in looking at the new angle."

Albuquerque Tribune, April 24, 1991

POLICE BLASTED ON ARQUETTE CASE

by Tribune staff

Two defense attorneys say Albuquerque police conducted a "shoddy" investigation into the shooting death of Kaitlyn Arquette.

The investigation focused on two innocent men and ignored a possible connection to Vietnamese gang activity, attorneys Joseph Riggs and Michael Davis said.

District Attorney Bob Schwartz said the decision to drop the charges was partially based on an investigation by Garcia's attorneys. They discovered that Arquette's relationship with a group of Vietnamese under investigation in a multimillion-dollar insurance scam may have led to her death.

Had the case gone to trial as scheduled next week, Davis said, "We were going to kill them on the stand."

He said the scam involved filing insurance claims on accidents with rental cars. A car rented with Arquette's credit card was involved in a California accident. After the accident a deposit of $1,500 appeared in Arquette's bank account.

Schwartz declined to comment on the quality of the police work.

Albuquerque Journal, June 9, 1992

MOTHER SURE BOOK WILL HELP SOLVE
ARQUETTE KILLING

by Colleen Heild

Albuquerque author Lois Duncan paid a visit to her daughter Kaitlyn's grave this past September. She brought along a copy of her latest manuscript–the moving chronicle of a mother's search for her child's killer.

It was Duncan's own story.

"I set it on the grave marker and told her, 'Happy birthday honey. This is my present to you. Mother is going to get your killer' ". . .

CHAPTER ONE

Ititled my book about our daughter's murder *One to the Wolves.* The title was suggested by our older son, Brett, who compared his sister's killers to wolves who invaded our family flock and made off with a lamb.

Now, on Kait's twenty-first birthday, I stood at her grave with the manuscript box in my hands.

"This is your present, honey," I told her. "Mother is going to get your killer." Even to my own ears, the statement sounded ludicrous. How was I going to keep that promise? Although I had written a number of fictional suspense novels, I knew nothing about how real murder investigations were conducted. I looked down at the grave marker and whispered aloud the inscription that Kait's oldest sister, Robin, had chosen for her epitaph, the heartbreaking lines that Mark Twain had written for his own daughter:

Warm summer sun, shine kindly here.
Warm southern wind, blow softly here.
Green sod above, lie light, lie light.
Good night, dear heart, good night, good night.

It was autumn now, although the season was veiled in Indian summer and the breeze that caressed my face was as soft and

Kait's Senior Picture. *(Courtesy: Kim Jew)*

unthreatening as the breeze that had ruffled Kait's hair on that sweet summer evening two years before when she left our home, never to return. I closed my eyes against the slanted rays of the afternoon sun and concentrated on picturing my daughter as I wanted to remember her—not as she had looked in the hospital with her head swathed in bandages, but healthy and strong, radiant with life and vitality, her green eyes sparkling with mischief and dreams of adventure.

That was how she had looked in her senior picture. She had selected that single picture out of dozens of poses.

"Are you sure you want to use that one?" I had asked her doubtfully. "It makes you look like you're hiding a naughty secret."

2

"It's how I want people to remember me," Kait had responded.

In retrospect, I thought, what a strange thing to say! Was it possible she had experienced some sort of premonition? Or was it only that the picture was startlingly glamorous?

I'd enclosed a copy of that photo in the box with the manuscript in case a publisher wanted to use it on the cover.

When I left the cemetery, I drove to the post office, arriving just before the "closed" sign went up on the door. It seemed terribly important that Kait's story be mailed on her birthday.

By the time I got back to the rented town house where my husband Don and I had been living since we had been driven out of our family home by threats to the rest of us following the arrest of three Hispanic suspects, Don had arrived home from work and was seated at the kitchen table, thumbing through the mail.

"Do you need help bringing in groceries?" he asked me.

"I haven't been shopping," I told him. "I've come from the post office. I mailed off the manuscript."

There was a moment's silence while Don digested that information.

Then he said, "Don't you think you're jumping the gun? Kait's story doesn't have an ending."

"Getting her story out there where people can read it may be our only chance of *getting* an ending," I said. "The police have washed their hands of the case, so the book won't hurt their investigation. Maybe it will bring informants out of the woodwork."

"Before that can happen you'll need to find a publisher," Don said. "Who's going to publish a true crime story that doesn't end with a conviction?"

When my agent received the manuscript, she had the same reaction.

Lois pores over information on Kait's case. Note the shelves stuffed
with files in the background of documents about the murder.
(Courtesy of Jennifer Bishop)

"I've read it," she told me. "It's a chilling story, but there isn't any
conclusion. All those unanswered questions are flapping in the wind.
Who was the triggerman? Did he act on his own or was he hired?
Is there a link between the Hispanic suspects and the Vietnamese
group? Did Kait truly have a secret second boyfriend named Rod
and, if so, where is he? What about all those psychic readings about
Kait's having seen a prominent citizen involved in a drug transaction
at a 'Desert Castle'? How can we expect anybody to accept *that*?"

"I can't create an ending when there isn't one," I said. "All I can do is describe events as they occurred. Please, won't you submit the story anyway?" I didn't think I could bear it if she told me she wouldn't.

"I'll submit it, but don't get your hopes up," my agent told me. "I'll try your usual publisher first, since they have a vested interest in your teenage suspense novels. But I have to warn you that your track record with young people isn't going to carry much weight with the adult department."

Several days later she phoned again.

"It looks like this actually may fly," she said with obvious surprise. "The editors are intrigued by the story, but they're leery of lawsuits. They don't want to commit to anything until their legal department gives them a go-ahead."

The following week I flew to New York to meet with the publisher's legal department, bringing with me suitcases containing the binders of documentation that had filled an entire bookcase in my home office. Those materials included the APD case file, transcripts of depositions, a transcript of the grand jury hearing at which Miguel Garcia and Juve Escobedo were indicted and a scrapbook filled with newspaper clippings that chronicled the downhill slide of the investigation.

I also brought dozens of audio tapes of phone conversations, since New Mexico was a state in which it was legal for one party to record phone calls without the second party's knowledge.

The publisher's attorney seemed particularly concerned about a police artist's sketches, based upon descriptions of two faces that psychic detective Noreen Renier described in a trance.

"Has anyone been able to identify those faces?" she asked me.

"The first sketch isn't of an actual person," I told her. "It's the hitman on the jacket of the British edition of my novel, *Don't Look Behind You*. Noreen believes Kait was trying to channel the message, 'It *wasn't* a random shooting! I was shot by a *drug dealer's hitman,* like the one in Mother's book!'"

"If it's just symbolic, then, that's okay," the attorney said. "But we definitely can't use the second sketch–the one the psychic says is the politician your daughter saw do drugs. If that happens to resemble a real person, there might be a libel suit."

Leaving the documentation with the legal department, I went to another office to meet with the senior editor and head publicist.

"If we publish this book we're going to want you to go on tour with it," the editor told me. "The subject is a natural for talk shows."

"I've never been on a talk show," I said nervously.

"Then we'll get you a media trainer," the publicist told me.

"A media trainer?" I wasn't familiar with the term.

"That's an expert who works with authors who are going on first-time promo tours. You'll be taught how to take control of an interview and deal with hecklers." Seeing my expression change from doubtful to terrified, he quickly switched to an alternate line of argument. "You wrote this book to motivate informants, didn't you?"

"Yes," I acknowledged.

"A promo tour will make that possible," the editor pointed out. "That visual exposure may be just what it takes to bring you the answers you're looking for. I'll be in touch with your agent to work out details. Oh, and one other thing–the book needs a stronger title."

"I like *One to the Wolves*!" I protested. That title held special meaning for me because it reminded me of an eerie picture of a wolf that Kait had created as an etching when she was ten. Was it possible, even back then, she was having nightmares about the "wolf" who would come for her eight years later?

"I'm afraid that's too subtle," the editor said. "We need a title that will jump out and grab people."

By the time I left her office, *One to the Wolves* had been re-titled *Who Killed My Daughter?*. I comforted myself with the thought that, if the time ever came that I wrote a sequel, I would use the "wolf" title.

I had also been assigned to a media trainer named Bill.

My training session consisted of an eight-hour marathon in Bill's New York office.

"I want to know all about what happened to your daughter," he told me. "Start at the beginning and tell me the story chronologically."

I braced myself and began.

"Kait stopped by our house at six that evening. I'm sure of the time, because *60 Minutes* had just come on. Kait had recently graduated from high school and gotten her own apartment, and she'd let her boyfriend, Dung Nguyen, move in with her.

"After the murder, her apartment manager told us that a lot had been going on that Kait hadn't shared with us. He said Kait was afraid of Dung's friends and had the locks changed to keep them out, but they broke a window and got in that way. Another time, she locked Dung out because he'd threatened her, and he kicked in the door. When she left our home on the night she was shot, Kait told us she was breaking up with Dung and was going to spend the evening with a new girlfriend named Susan Smith*, and if Dung called trying to find her—"

Bill lifted his hand to signal me to stop.

"Let's take it from the top," he said. "You need to tighten that up. In your first sentence, identify Kait by name and say where and

7

Etching created by Kait Arquette at age 10.

when she was shot. In your second sentence, state the problem you have with the investigation. Save the details for later."

I drew a deep breath and started over.

"In July, 1989, our daughter, Kaitlyn Arquette, was murdered in Albuquerque, New Mexico." I glanced at Bill for confirmation, and he nodded his approval. "The police called the shooting a random drive-by, but our family is convinced Kait was killed because she was getting ready to blow the whistle on interstate crime."

My detailed rendition of the story took forty-two minutes and left me emotionally exhausted.

"Pretty good," Bill said. "Now, let's try it again."

"Again?" I exclaimed incredulously.

"Most shows won't allow you anywhere near that much time," Bill said. "Let's say you're on a show that allows you only ten minutes. How are you going to condense this to fit that time frame?"

We worked the story down to ten minutes. Then, to five minutes. And, finally, to three minutes. One hundred and eighty seconds to describe the circumstances of Kait's murder and explain

Dung Nguyen. *(Photo by Kaitlyn Arquette)*

9

why we believed the shooting was premeditated.

We broke for a hurried lunch and returned for "the hard part."

"How many TV appearances have you done?" Bill asked me.

"None, except for a couple of local newscasts."

"Then we'll need to start you from scratch. Let's move into the studio."

The room that connected to Bill's office was arranged like a stage set. He placed me in a chair, directed lights at my face, and started a camera rolling. Now, in addition to worrying about the content of the story, I had to be concerned about the direction of my eyes, the intensity of my expression and the angle of my head.

"Keep your chin down," Bill directed. "Tilting your head like that makes you appear unapproachable. Keep your gestures at chest level so your hands don't come between your face and the camera. And if you're going to cross your legs, do it at the ankles."

Toward the end of the day we got to the phone-in programs. Bill played devil's advocate and goaded me with the types of questions he said I could expect from a call-in audience.

I had grown so accustomed to his empathetic interview style that this new approach came as a shock.

"Mrs. Arquette—or *Ms. Duncan*, or whatever you want to call yourself—as a member of the Police Benevolent Society, I'm shocked and offended by your criticism of our boys in blue. Why would they want to cover up for an Asian crime ring?"

"That's what we'd like to know!" I shot back. "We trusted the police! We believed in those shows on television where they follow up on every bit of evidence, and take statements from all witnesses and suspects, and write honest reports—"

"No!" Bill broke in. "That's not the way to respond. If you let yourself be provoked into a display of anger you'll weaken your credibility."

"Then how do I answer a question like that one?"

"Take the high road," Bill told me. "State your position with dignity in as few words as possible and try not to sound accusatory. Let's try it again." He repeated the question in exactly the same words.

"I don't want to believe they're 'covering up,'" I responded in a gentler voice. "Whenever Dung was interviewed, he acted like he could hardly speak English. Maybe that scared the cops off. On the other hand, the case detective told us that they have a Vietnamese consultant. We don't understand why he wasn't called in for those interviews."

The barrage of challenging questions continued until it was time for me to leave for the airport.

"You're going to do just fine," Bill said reassuringly as he handed me the video of our training session. "Take this home and analyze it. You'll learn a lot by viewing yourself objectively. If you get up-tight about a particular show, feel free to call me."

The traffic was lighter than expected, and my cab driver got me to the airport with time to spare. I checked my luggage, went to the gate and took a seat in the crowded waiting area. I had a paperback book in my purse but was too tired to read it. Instead, I replayed the day over and over in my mind, cringing at the memory of the hideous questions Bill had hurled at me in his well-intentioned effort to prepare me for the worst that call-in viewers could dish out.

"How could you let your daughter date somebody of another race?"

"What kind of slut was she to let her boyfriend move in with her?"

"Why can't you put this unfortunate event behind you and get on with your life? You and your husband still have four living children. That should be enough for anybody."

His final question had been especially devastating.

"Why would a clean-cut honor student—who had never been in trouble with the law, who didn't do drugs, who wouldn't even smoke a cigarette—become involved with an organized crime ring?"

I'd asked myself that question a thousand times and still hadn't found an answer.

Shortly after the shooting, Kait's sister, Robin, had said to me, "Aside from losing Kait, the worst thing about this nightmare is knowing that she never had a chance to make her life meaningful. She had so many dreams for the future, and she couldn't fulfill them. I can't bear the thought that Kait died an empty death."

So far, I had managed to deal with my personal agony by pouring our on-going horror story onto paper. But what would I do with my pain now that the book was completed and I no longer had that outlet?

A wave of dizziness struck me, and the world became suddenly diffused as if a movie projector had slipped out of focus. My ears were filled with the sound of my accelerated heartbeat, and I gripped the arms of my seat to keep from falling out of my chair. The anxiety attack seemed to last for no more than a minute, but when I opened my eyes I found that the waiting room was empty. I glanced about me in bewilderment—where had all the people gone? Then I looked at my watch and discovered that over half an hour had passed since I last had been conscious of the world around me.

I got up and went over to the counter.

"Where is everybody?" I asked the attendant. "Has the gate been changed?"

"No, ma'am," he said with a smirk.

"So, how late is the flight?"

"It was right on time," he told me. "It took off ten minutes ago just like it was supposed to."

"But I didn't hear you call it!"

"That's your problem, lady. Fifty people walked right over your feet to get on it and you just sat there."

That was when I realized that my kind media trainer had overestimated my resilience. I was *not* going to be "just fine."

CHAPTER TWO

When I finally got back to Albuquerque on a much later flight, Don and I were faced with a decision that we had not expected to have to make for years. We knew that, when my book was published, the charming Southwestern city where we had lived for our whole married life would never be home to us again.

"We need to get out of here before the book comes out," Don said. "There's bound to be retaliation."

"From the Vietnamese?"

"That's possible, of course, but we also could be in danger from the Hispanic suspects. When the DA dropped charges against Miguel Garcia, he and his friends thought they were off the hook. Now your book will come out, speculating that they possibly were hired hit men. They won't be happy about that."

"The police are the ones I'm worried about," I said.

Several of my former journalism students at the University of New Mexico were now reporters for local newspapers and had told me disturbing stories about their experiences with police harassment when they wrote articles that portrayed the department unfavorably. Accusations of police brutality were becoming increasingly common in Albuquerque, and the number of killings by police was reportedly far above the norm for a city that size.

One highly publicized police shooting was engraved on my

memory because it occurred the same year Kait was shot. Peter Klunck, a small time drug dealer, had been chased down and shot to death by police officers on the morning of the day Peter was scheduled for a court appearance. Matt Griffin, the cop who fired the death shot, claimed self-defense, although several witnesses, including a fellow officer, reported Peter was unarmed, and Peter's parents were convinced the killing was premeditated.

The police department rallied in defense of Griffin, who was kept on the force until July of that same year when he killed a man who caught him hot-wiring a car. One week before Kait's murder, Matt Griffin was revealed to be the "Ninja Bandit," a notorious bank robber. Despite that revelation, police remained firm in their contention that Peter's parents were slanderous troublemakers who had no right to question Griffin's motive for shooting their son.

The longer Don and I discussed the possible ramifications of the book's publication, the more uneasy we became. After hashing it over, we decided not to take chances, so Don applied for early retirement, and we bought a secondhand fifth-wheel trailer. When the book was released, we planned to evacuate the town house and move into the trailer at a campground outside the city limits.

But the book was not scheduled for publication until spring, which meant that, although Don continued to put in his usual long hours at the office, my own life was on hold. I was still under contract to write the last of three suspense novels, only two of which had been completed at the time of Kait's death, but I found it impossible to create a fictional murder mystery when my mind would not focus on anything other than our real one.

So, with nothing to do but kill time, I dutifully devoted my days to analyzing talk shows. I had never before watched daytime

15

television, and I found myself mesmerized by the subject matter and the wildly contrasting participants. The guests on the *Joan Rivers Show* were a classy lot and obviously most had had media training. *The Maury Povitch Show* was not for the faint of heart, what with all the satanic cultists and serial killers, but Maury had a nice smile. Oprah Winfrey and Phil Donahue ran opposite each, so I took turns switching back and forth. *The Donahue Show* tended to intimidate me, as Phil's guests were often so bizarre, and the studio audience went straight for the jugular. The Oprah audience was kinder, perhaps as a reflection of Oprah herself, who seemed like the sort of person who would be fun at a party. I also developed warm feelings for Sally Jessy Raphael, who appeared sincerely sympathetic to the parade of agonized bigamists, transvestites, and adult-children-of-dysfunctional-parents, who trooped on and off the set to the cheers and applause of a surprisingly youthful audience.

At the end of each "workday" of TV viewing, I would replay Bill's training video and compare my pathetic performance to those I had just witnessed. Every time, I found new things to worry about. My voice was either too flat or too shrilly emotional; I paused too long between sentences or jabbered so nervously that I ran out of breath; I gestured too much or, conversely, clenched my hands together in my lap in a knot of rigidity that made me appear catatonic. And, whenever I described the hours at Kait's bedside, holding her hand and waiting for her to die, I started to gasp as if I had asthma.

Since Don's last day of work was the tenth of December, we decided to take the trailer on a maiden voyage to spend the holidays with our second daughter, Kerry, and her family. In a campground in Texas it quickly became apparent why we had gotten such a good deal on the trailer. It rained non-stop all Christmas week, and the roof sprung so many leaks that we felt as if we were sleeping in a shower stall. On top of that, our plumbing performed some sort of reflux action that sent floods of water gushing out of the sink and toilet to join forces with the pools of rainwater. The ratty shag carpet soaked up the liquid like a blotter and emitted a pungent odor of stale beer and cat urine that told us more about the former owners of the trailer than we wanted to know.

Kerry tried to make our visit a festive one, but the going was rough for her. Both our little granddaughters had ear infections, our son-in-law had just learned that his job was being terminated, and Kerry herself was in her ninth month of pregnancy. Despite our best efforts, we never quite got the holidays up and rolling. As the baby of the family, Kait had been the pivot of Christmas, and memories of happier times overwhelmed us.

"Remember when she wrapped up all her old toys and put them under the tree so she would have more packages to open than Donnie?"

"Remember when she baked pies and forgot to put in sugar?"

"Remember when we took her to see *The Nutcracker*, and she brought the hamsters in her purse so they could see the Mouse King?"

I remember, I responded silently. Oh, yes, I remember.

I remembered the chubby three-year-old, still damp from her bath, who snuggled on Don's lap as he read her *The Night Before Christmas*. I remembered the gregarious ten-year-old who sang Christmas carols off key as she lined the driveway with luminarias. I remembered the starry-eyed teenager on the last Christmas Eve of her life, filling a stocking for her boyfriend—"Dung says they don't have Christmas stockings in Vietnam. I'm going to sneak over and hang this on his door knob."

Kait and Donnie, gleefully listening as Don reads a Christmas story.

(Arquette family photo)

Precariously balanced on an emotional seesaw that could plunge me into depression with the slightest bit of overload, I flipped over the edge on the day I made a last minute dash to a department store to pick up a present that Kerry had placed on layaway. As I stood waiting for the over-worked salesgirl to bring out the package, I heard a girl's voice call, "Mother!"

"Yes?" I responded automatically, and turned to see a pretty blond teenager pull a blouse from a rack and hold it up in front of her.

"This is the one you ought to buy!" she announced emphatically

Baby Kait, with Lois during an innocent time. *(Arquette family photo)*

Kait at about age three, beneath the Christmas tree. *(Arquette family photo)*

19

Kait at age four, watering flowers in the family garden.

(Arquette family photo)

Kait at age six, playing softball. *(Arquette family photo)*

Kait at age eight. *(Arquette family photo)*

Donnie, Lois, Don and Kait, on a family trip to Hawaii.
(Arquette family photo)

to the middle-aged woman standing next to her. "It's in your colors!"

"Those are *your* colors!" the woman responded, laughing. "You only want me to buy that so you can borrow it!"

Her daughter joined in the laughter. "Can't blame me for trying! Oh, Mother, look—isn't that the coolest jacket!"

She grabbed the woman's hand and dragged her across the aisle to another rack of clothing, and a scene from the past came rushing back to me.

It was the Mother's Day that Kait was twelve, and she announced to me at breakfast that she had a very special gift for me.

"I've neglected you lately," she said solemnly. "I've been so busy that I haven't scheduled enough time for you. To make up for that, I'm going to spend the whole day with you." She smiled at my look of bewilderment. "*That's* your present, Mother! I'm going to spend every minute of this entire day with you. What shall we do first?"

"That sounds wonderful, honey," I responded in amusement, "but I'm afraid I have work to do." I was running behind on an article assignment and had expected to devote the day to getting it finished.

"That's all right," Kait said agreeably. "I'll entertain you while you write. Then we can go out to lunch and to a movie and then we can go someplace expensive to shop for a blouse or something. You're much too old to buy all your clothes at Wal-Mart."

The idea of trying to write with a chattering parakeet perched next to me was inconceivable, so I reluctantly put my assignment on hold and went out to "do the town" with Kait. We had lunch at the Chic-Fil-A (Kait's favorite eatery); saw a movie with Nicholas Cage (Kait's favorite actor); and ended up buying me a blouse (in Kait's favorite colors). Since Kait had forgotten to bring money, I picked up the tab.

"Did you like your present?" she chirped as we walked hand-in-hand to the parking lot. "Wasn't it special to get to spend so much time with me?"

"It certainly was," I told her, trying not to dwell upon the fact that I would have to work half the night to finish the article.

Oh, dear God, if only I could have that day back again! The sense of loss that struck me was so intense that I thought for a moment I might die of it. Where was that orange and yellow blouse today?

24

Hanging at the back of my closet at the town house? On a rack at the Goodwill Thrift Store? Or was it nothing but a sun-bleached rag on a shelf in a corner of the laundry room of the home we had vacated? Why hadn't I cherished it, slept with it under my pillow or, at the very least, worn it to the funeral?

Did you like your present?

"It was a wonderful present," I whispered now. "It was the most wonderful present in the world—the chance to spend a whole day with you."

On New Year's Day the inevitable finally happened, and my body followed the path of my careening emotions. I was standing in Kerry's kitchen, leaning over to take a pan of chicken out of the oven, when I discovered that my left hand wouldn't close around the door handle. Then my left arm went limp. I tried to call out to the family, who were already gathered at the dinner table, but the words came out in a garble.

What I was trying to say was, "I think I've had a stroke!"

On the way to the hospital I got my speech back and dictated a living will.

Later that night I became able to move my arm and hand. As I lay in the hospital bed, clenching and re-clenching my left fist in a frenzied effort to reassure myself that I could still do so, a nurse kept popping in to ask if I could swallow. I quickly realized that swallowing was some kind of test so, of course, my mouth dried up every time the nurse appeared. In between her visits I manufactured saliva, which I surreptitiously stockpiled in the crevices of my mouth so that when she next materialized I could demonstrate my swallowing skills.

"Do you understand that you've had a stroke?" she asked me.

I assured her that I did.

"So what is your emotional state?" she continued, consulting her checklist. "You have four choices—denial, fear, anger, and acceptance."

"Acceptance," I said.

She raised her eyes from the list and regarded me suspiciously.

"You haven't had time enough for acceptance."

"Anger?" I suggested, although I didn't feel angry. There was nothing and no one to be angry with except Fate, and I knew for a fact that Fate dealt harsher blows than this one.

The nurse looked relieved and checked the square beside "anger."

The shock of seeing me babbling and drooling in her kitchen had driven Kerry into labor and, while I was getting my brain scanned, she gave birth two floors below me. I emerged from the MRI tube to find Don waiting with a wheelchair to take me down to meet our first grandson, Ryan Duncan.

I remained in the hospital four days and had a myriad of tests which revealed no overt cause for a stroke. I was in seemingly good health.

"There's no good reason for a non-smoking, middle-aged woman to suffer a stroke," one doctor said accusingly. "You are going to have to learn to cope better with stress and to stop letting life's little problems become major issues for you."

The only obvious after-effects of the "TIA," as the doctors were now calling it, was that my smile was lopsided and my left hand didn't type as fast as my right one. However it had triggered neurological problems. I would get weak and nauseous, see flashing psychedelic lights, and experience the sensation of plunging down an elevator shaft.

The idea of going on the road in such a condition was terrifying, and for the first time I found myself questioning whether it was worth it. I'd written a freaky book, a book with no ending, an outpouring of grief and frustration and accusations of forms of crime that police officers didn't think existed. Why would anyone read such a book, much less take it seriously? Why would they take *me* seriously when I appeared on their TV screens, even if I kept my chin down and crossed my legs at the ankles? What if I blacked out on camera or my speech became garbled? Viewers would think I was drunk.

A torrent of hopelessness swept over me and, like a child groping for a security blanket, I reached out to our hometown psychic, Betty Muench.

Kait's sister, Robin, had first visited Betty, without our knowledge, after reading in the paper that Dung had stabbed himself. Robin wanted to know what had spurred that action—grief or guilt?

Ignoring our skeptical reaction when she told us what she had done, she had handed Don and me four single spaced typewritten pages that described Dung's relationship with Kait and some of the circumstances that led to the shooting.

That reading, which Betty had done without charge, contained information that was new to us but much of which would later prove to be accurate. About Dung, it said, *"It is not as if he will have been the one to do this, but he will seem to know who did it."* Betty had since done several other readings for us, and Don and I had come to accept the validity of her gift, even if we didn't understand it.

Now I phoned her and said, "I have a question for you. I've written a book about Kait's murder and I need to know what the prospects are for its success."

Betty asked me the name of the book, and I told her the title that

27

the publisher had selected. Then I sat and listened to the rattle of her typewriter as she appeared to be taking dictation from some source that only she could hear.

After she completed the reading, she read it aloud:

QUESTION: WHAT IS THE POTENTIAL FOR LOIS'S BOOK, WHO KILLED MY DAUGHTER?

ANSWER: *There is this energy that shows that this work is to fulfill its purpose. This will not have been only to find the murderer, but this will have also been a tribute by this one mother to this one child, and this will go beyond this lifetime.*

There will be in this a potential which will reach out to many people in many different ways. There will be people who will find affinity in the loss of a child, and others who will find affinity in the inappropriate behaviors of police and crime solvers. There will come much attention to this aspect of the book all over the country, and much will come out of that for the betterment of policemen all over.

There is much that Kait can say about all this energy that has been expended on her behalf, and she will know that all is being done that can be done at this time.

*There is an assurance in Kait that there will come this which will seem to put **the collar on the wolf** who will have been after her. **There will be this image of a kind of wild wolf with something on its neck as it howls with its neck up in the air.** There is a sense of message which will show that there is knowing in her that this will be done and that the wolf will come into forms of justice which Lois and all her family and friends will bear witness to. There will be fear, and a*

28

mistake will be made, and there will be in the minds of all sensible beings the knowing that the efforts of Lois in this will have been the target for this justice.

There is a sense of relief and relaxation in Kait—much warmth and softness in her now.

Mom, I love you. Look out for the walker, the innocent walker, who does more than walk.

"I gather from this that Kait is still very much a part of the action," Betty told me. "She hasn't moved on to other realms yet. I wouldn't be surprised if she was standing at your shoulder, watching you write your book."

"I can believe that," I said quietly.

For Betty didn't know—nor did anyone else on this earth plane other than Don and my editor—that the original title for my book had been *One to the Wolves.*

CHAPTER THREE

The book hit the city of Albuquerque like a nuclear explosion. One bookstore that had placed an order for one hundred copies sold them all within hours and frantically wired the warehouse for another shipment. TV newscasts showed customers scrambling for the last copies on the shelves, and newspaper headlines screamed "Sloppy Police Work Frustrated Duncan" and "Mother Relentlessly Searches for the Awful Truth."

"This book is sure to offend some readers," said an article in the *Albuquerque Tribune*. "Albuquerque police are portrayed as a bunch of bureaucratic bunglers, the District Attorney's Office as uncaring prosecutors . . . Each time Arquette's family uncovered additional information that suggested her death was no accident, it would be turned over to the police. But, Duncan wrote, the information never went anywhere because police insisted the shooting was random."

Initially the police declined to comment, saying they could not discuss the investigation because it was on-going. A day or so later they changed their minds. The deputy chief of investigations told reporters, "The case is still open, but there's no active investigation." Asked whether he had read the book, he responded, "No, I don't read fiction." He said the police department stood by their investigation as thorough and professional and "we checked out every lead there was."

There was also reaction to the book from the Vietnamese. When we took up residence in the camper, we had subscribed to an answering service, and our voice mail contained threats from people with Vietnamese accents. One was a woman whose observations about our family were of such a personal nature that it was obvious that she had been coached by somebody who knew us.

The promotion tour was launched in New York, and I made my TV debut on *Good Morning, America*. When I arrived at the studio I made the unsettling discovery that I would be sharing the segment with members of New Mexico law enforcement who had been taped in advance by the CBS affiliate in Albuquerque.

"Police say it is unlikely there will ever be another arrest," said the narrator, shown standing at the intersection where Kait was shot. "Police say they know who killed Kaitlyn, but without reliable witnesses it's a case that will not hold up in court."

The next face to fill the screen was that of a captain from APD.

"I think our people did an excellent job," he said proudly. "The Vietnamese angle was extensively looked into. We were aware of that soon after the homicide occurred. We could find no tie to the homicide with any Vietnamese gang."

Then, onto the screen popped the face of District Attorney Bob Schwartz.

"Did the police blow the investigation?" the reporter asked him.

"No," Schwartz said. "This case was victimized by the witnesses in the case." His voice took on a note of sadness. "I have seen other parents who have suffered the worst pain imaginable . . . they need to blame someone and they typically will blame the system."

"What do you want to say in response to what you just heard?" the hostess, Joan Lundon, asked me as my face replaced Schwartz's

31

on the monitor.

In deference to Bill's instructions to "take the high road," I tried to respond diplomatically.

"When people in authority are backed to the wall it's common for them to be defensive about it," I said. "Bob Schwartz, as far as I know, is an ethical man, but being in the position he is as district attorney, all he had to go on was what was in the police reports. I think there are things that Bob Schwartz wasn't aware of."

"Good luck to you, Lois Duncan."

Mercifully it was over, and I knew in my heart that it had been a disaster. The last thing I had expected was that on my very first interview I would be forced to respond to statements from Albuquerque law enforcement. The police captain had made me seem like a paranoid liar, alleging that there was Asian gang activity when none existed, and the district attorney had issued the coup de grace by portraying me as a woman so deranged by grief that she was attacking the very people who were trying to help her.

I returned to the hotel, so embarrassed and discouraged that all I wanted to do was cry.

The phone in my room was ringing when I entered my room.

It was the assistant publicist who had arranged the tour.

"We're already getting calls about the program," she told me. "Producers from several major talk shows are interested in interviewing you, and we've had a firm invitation from *Larry King Live*. You're going to be on that show a week from Tuesday."

"But it was a fiasco!" I exclaimed. "That captain said the Vietnamese angle was thoroughly investigated, and the district attorney—"

"That's what hooked their interest!" the publicist broke in. "A grief stricken mother isn't interesting unless there's conflict. Larry

32

King is going to let you spar with the district attorney via satellite."

"He's *what*?" I gasped in horror. The talking heads on *Good Morning, America* had been intimidating enough, but at least I had been able to respond without interacting.   A debate with the district attorney was out of the question. Not only was Schwartz a slick and experienced prosecutor, he had a second persona as a stand-up comedian, known for his barbed wit and his ability to verbally decapitate opponents.

"I can't do it," I said. "There's no way I can 'spar' with Bob Schwartz."

"You can't turn this down," the publicist told me. "*Larry King* is one of the most popular shows on television. Your book will get tremendous national exposure."

The week that followed passed in a blur of newspaper, radio and television interviews. Every evening I would get on a plane and fly to a different city, check into a hotel, sleep for a few hours, and get up to face a new round of appearances. New York, Connecticut, New Jersey, Massachusetts, Ohio and Michigan slid past without making a dent in my memory. I was so focused upon the frightening prospect of appearing on *Larry King Live* with Bob Schwartz flitting on and off the screen that I couldn't think of anything else. Then, the publicist called with a piece of truly chilling news. Rather than appearing by satellite, Schwartz had now decided to fly to Washington D.C. to do the show live.

The publicist was delighted. What a treat for the viewers! They would get to watch the razor tongued district attorney humiliate me in person!

That night, in desperation, I sat down with a pencil and hotel stationary and started mapping out a battle plan. I was painfully aware that I lacked the DA's gift for showmanship, but I did have one thing going for me—I knew more about the case than he did. I could raise issues concerning the investigation that Schwartz very likely knew nothing about.

I vowed to myself that I was not going to continue to be cast as a grief-crazed housewife creating monsters out of dust balls. I would come to the show armed with facts so inarguable and incriminating that APD's handling of the case would be indefensible.

I arrived in Washington D.C. at 5 p.m. on June 9, after a full day of radio and television interviews in Detroit. I checked into my hotel, pressed some clothes to wear on the show, and had just begun to review my sheaf of notes when the phone rang.

It was Don calling from Albuquerque.

"Betty just sent us another reading," he told me. "I think you'd do well to go easy on APD tonight."

"You can't mean that!" I exclaimed. "This is our one big chance to get all our information out there!"

"You can't afford to blast the police," Don said. "This reading says Kait's killers eventually will turn on each other and Dung will spill his guts. We're going to need the police to make the arrests. If you embarrass them, you may alienate them so badly that they'll bury all the tips this show may generate."

"They probably don't watch *Larry King Live*," I said. "Doesn't it come on opposite one of those cop shows?"

"Everybody in Albuquerque will be watching it tonight," Don said. "All the TV stations have interviewed Schwartz, and there's a piece in tonight's *Tribune* that says you and he are 'bringing new life to what police describe as a dead murder investigation.'"

"But my whole reason for being on the show—"

"Is to point out the problems with the case," Don completed my sentence. "You can still accomplish that, but let Larry King challenge Schwartz. Lois, this reading is a step-by-step description of exactly how the case is going to develop. I'll FAX it to your next hotel. For now, just take my word that you need to go easy."

I replaced the receiver on the hook and gazed uncertainly at my notes. So many of Betty's predictions had come to pass that it was hard to shrug off this one, especially when Don appeared to be taking it so seriously. I wadded up my game plan and tossed it into the wastebasket. Then I took the elevator down to the lobby and went outside, where a studio limousine awaited me.

"There's another guest too," I told the driver. "I guess he hasn't come down yet."

"The guests on *Larry King* take separate limos," the driver said.

"I don't see him out here waiting for one," I said doubtfully, scanning the sidewalk for the sight of the bushy moustache that was the district attorney's distinctive trademark.

"They put him at a different hotel," the driver told me. "They want their guests to battle on the set, not in a hotel lobby."

When I signed in at the studio, Schwartz's signature was on the line above mine, so I knew that he had arrived, although I still saw no sign of him. After a stint in the make-up room, I was assigned to a small private waiting room where a television set showed Larry King interviewing his first set of guests. After each commercial break the jacket of my book would flash across the screen and Kait's mischievous face would twinkle at me and disappear again.

There was a self-conscious cough behind me, and I turned to see the district attorney standing in the doorway, his face as plastered with pancake make-up as mine was.

35

"I just thought I'd check and see what I should call you on the show," he said. "Do you prefer to be 'Ms. Duncan' or 'Mrs. Arquette'?"

"Call me 'Lois,' of course," I said. "May I call you 'Bob'?"

Before he could respond, a hand appeared out of nowhere, grabbed Schwartz by the collar and yanked him out of view. A woman's head replaced his in the doorway.

"You are not to speak to each other before the show," she told me.

The woman vanished and came back several minutes later to escort me to the set. As she led me down the hall we passed a second waiting room identical to mine where Bob Schwartz sat in isolation in front of another TV set. He glanced up as I passed the open door, and I gave him a thumbs-up sign, which I hoped he wouldn't misinterpret. He responded with a nod and a wave.

A commercial was in progress as I was ushered onto the set, seated at a table, and equipped with a lapel mike. There was a surrealistic quality about the experience. There, across the table from me, sat Larry King—*live!*—a big flesh and blood replica of the miniature face I was accustomed to seeing on our TV screen, and there was no way to escape by switching channels.

"So, your name is—" Larry King consulted his notes—"your name is Lois Duncan and—your daughter was *murdered?*"

"Yes." I was bewildered by the question. Wasn't that why I'd been asked to appear on the show?

"Let's see," he continued, still scanning the notes. "Her name was Kaitlyn—*Arquette?* Why do you have different last names? Was your daughter married?"

"Of course not," I said. "Kait was only a teenager. My married name is Arquette, the same as hers. Lois Duncan is my pen name."

The awful truth hit me—*Larry King did not appear to have read the book!* This TV Superstar, whom Don had perceived as my knight-in-shining-armor, was preparing to conduct an in-depth interview about a murder investigation that he seemed to know little about. There was no way he could challenge Bob Schwartz with penetrating questions if he wasn't aware of the issues!

The commercial ended, and King's face appeared on the monitor.

"It's every mother's worst nightmare, and Lois Duncan is living it," King said, gazing intently into the camera lens. "One night in July 1989, eighteen-year-old Kaitlyn Arquette was brutally murdered during a high speed chase in Albuquerque, New Mexico. Police dismiss the case as a random shooting, but Kaitlyn's mother, Lois Duncan, felt that her daughter's death was no accident and launched an exhaustive search for the truth."

I stared at him in amazement, terribly impressed. Nobody would have guessed that he was coming out of nowhere.

His notes ran out and he turned to me for assistance.

"What happened in July of 1989?"

I gave a short account of the shooting, wording my statements with care so as not to appear to be criticizing anyone in law enforcement.

There was another commercial break, during which Schwartz was hustled onto the set to take a seat next to me.

"What do you make of all this, Bob?" King asked him.

"The police investigation is almost a mirror image of what's in Lois Duncan's book," Bob Schwartz admitted. "The police investigation tells us who did it, what happened, how it happened, what it doesn't tell us is why it happened. And as a prosecutor you learn to quit trying to understand *why* people get killed and just accept it."

"What do you mean it tells us who did it?"

"It tells us who most likely did it."

"But you can't prove it?"

"No, we can't prove it."

"Who, in your opinion, most likely did it?"

"The two young men who were arrested for the crime."

"And it may have been murder-for-hire?"

"No, we don't believe that," Schwartz said. "Quite frankly, I wouldn't hire these guys to mow my lawn, much less mow down a young woman in Albuquerque."

"So it's termed what now?"

"It is an open investigation. It is dormant at the moment. We are hoping another lead will pop up. That's what ultimately led me to drop the charges, because if we took a shot at this I was convinced we would have lost. There were two major problems. One was that the witnesses who originally put the case together for us started back pedaling and became unusable. The other was that the defense attorneys had gotten onto this Vietnamese connection, which was a much better motive for the killing than random shooting. It's a good motive. You dangle a good motive in front of a jury, and we thought that would foreclose the case."

King turned to me. "What do you want him to do, Lois?"

I choked back the obvious response and determinedly took the high road.

"Well, I think Bob will be very open to any new information that comes in," I said demurely. "What I'm hoping the book will do— what Bob and I are both hoping will be accomplished here tonight— is that people who hear this story will be motivated to come forward with some concrete information that the police can use."

"You're not angry at Bob and the police?"

"No, I'm not angry at Bob," I said. I could not bring myself to go further than that.

"You feel Bob was right in not going ahead with the trial?"

"He had no choice," I said. "And I think the police did a very good job as far as making the arrests. I think where the police may have fallen down—"

I described how the police had refused to check out the calls made from Kait's apartment to California on the night Kait died, when that apartment should have been unoccupied.

Schwartz sidestepped that issue as if it never had been raised, asserting with conviction that the police had "followed every leaf in the wind."

King seemed irritated that he was not getting a rise out of either of us.

"What do you think about that book she wrote?" he demanded of Schwartz.

"It's a good book," Schwartz conceded.

After that we took phone calls, mostly from people in Albuquerque who posed a variety of questions, including whether Schwartz was using publicity surrounding the case to aid his reelection campaign. Schwartz said he was not.

It was the final call of the evening that took us by surprise.

"What about the drugs?" a male voice demanded. "Why aren't you talking about *that*?"

Schwartz quickly assured the caller that the shooting could not have been anything but "random."

At the end of the show King thanked us politely for participating, although I suspected that he was disappointed in our performance.

As we left the set, Schwartz asked me to autograph his copy of my book. Then, before I could suggest that the two of us go somewhere for a drink or coffee, we were dragged off in opposite directions to be whisked away in his-and-hers limos to separate hotels. My chance for a private chat with the district attorney, to fill him in on all the facts he wasn't aware of, had been snatched away from me before I could reach out and grab for it.

Back in my room, I lay awake for hours, rerunning the evening's dialogue in my mind, disgusted with myself for having allowed Don to convince me to give such a tepid presentation. When I realized that Larry King was not going to serve as our champion, why hadn't I swung back to Plan One? Schwartz obviously had not been given the true facts. What would have happened, I now asked myself, if I had challenged him with those? What if I had responded to Larry King's question, "What do you want Bob to do, Lois!" with the shriek of fury and frustration that had been threatening to strangle me—*"If, as Bob says, the Vietnamese connection is a much better motive for the killing than random shooting, I want him to force the police to* investigate *that probability!"*

I wallowed in that thought for a moment and then had to acknowledge the possibility that it could have finished off what was left of my credibility. If Schwartz was sincerely convinced that the police investigation was a thorough one, he would have labeled my accusations ridiculous, and because of his official position his statements would have carried more weight than those of a distraught mother driven crazy by bereavement.

As I finally drifted off, serenaded by flushing toilets and gushing showers as my next-room neighbors prepared to go down to breakfast, I consoled myself with the thought that Bob Schwartz did have a copy of the book, and, unlike Larry King, he apparently had read it. I wanted to believe that I had seen a glimmer of respect in his eyes as we maintained our dignity under the most stressful of circumstances.

Maybe, I thought hopefully, after taking a careful look at the flaws in the police investigation, the district attorney would become an ally.

Yet one question continued to nag at me even as I slid into sleep. Why had Bob Schwartz, an astute and aggressive prosecutor, so quickly dismissed the idea that Kait's murder might be drug related? Why hadn't he asked some questions and invited a discussion? That caller had sounded as if he might have had crucial information.

If only I'd taken the initiative and asked questions of my own! Hindsight was always 20-20.

If the mere suggestion of a possible link between an Asian criminal group and political VIPs involved in the New Mexico drug scene had been enough to cause the district attorney to shy away from it, could that have been what had blocked the police investigation?

CHAPTER FOUR

Albuquerque Journal, July 11, 1992

MY 15 MINUTES OF FAME PAID WELL, DA SCHWARTZ SAYS

Bernalillo County District Attorney Bob Schwartz gets the "Working Smarter" award of the year.

"I've never been paid so well for 15 minutes of work," Schwartz joked of his appearance on CNN's "Larry King Live" show.

King invited Schwartz and Albuquerque author Lois Duncan to discuss the 1989 murder of Duncan's 18-year-old daughter, Kaitlyn Arquette.

"Ordinarily I work real cheap," Schwartz said, laughing. His salary is $67,500 a year, which he says breaks down to an hourly salary in the upper $30s or low $40s. Of course, Schwartz said, he didn't actually get paid to be on the show. But all his expenses were covered, including his plane ticket, cab fare, and two nights in the Bellevue Hotel on Capitol Hill. . . .

As a bonus, publicity-savvy Schwartz gained international exposure.

In an impromptu phone interview last week, Schwartz reiterated that he didn't do the show for political or campaign reasons.

"But did I mind the exposure? Of course not. I hope it comes in

handy. You never know."
Already he has received lots of back-pats from Albuquerqueans.

While Bob was being congratulated back in Albuquerque, I proceeded on to Chicago where the FAX of Betty's new reading was waiting for me. I now understood why Don had reacted so strongly, for it predicted a time when those around Dung would *"show how dangerous they truly are, and they will turn on one another. At that time Dung will be in great danger, and before he will depart to parts unknown he will tell the whole story and it will be accepted. The mysteries will be cleared up in such a professional manner as to surprise those who will complete them about themselves. . . . There will come a kind of crackdown on certain activities, and this will lead to the capture of all those who will seem to have missed the loop in all this. The stage is set!"*

However, I noted that the reading did not specify that the investigators would be local law enforcement. They might be DEA or FBI agents.

When Don phoned me that night he had something new to tell me.

"I had a call from a man who said Susan Smith was desperate to talk to me," he said. "He gave me an out-of-state phone number and told me to call her. When I did, she had only one topic on her mind—the time Kait got to her house. In *Who Killed My Daughter?* you quoted her as saying Kait got there at nine-thirty. Susan seemed frantic to convince me she got there at seven-thirty."

"Who was the man who called you?" I asked.

"He wouldn't identify himself. And another odd thing—he

didn't call our home number and leave a message on our voice mail. He phoned the office here at the campground."

"But nobody knows where we parked the trailer!" I exclaimed. "How did he find you?"

"I can only imagine that he was a cop," Don said. "They have ways of tracking people down. Yet, why would Susan relay her message through a cop in order to refute the police reports?"

The promo tour was a magnificently orchestrated road show that whisked me in and out of one location after another. Eventually a day came when I woke up in the morning and had to call down to the desk to find out where I was. I did not use the deadbolts on the doors of my hotel rooms in case I had another stroke and needed medical attention. I also obeyed Kait's instructions, via Betty's reading, to keep a vigilant eye out for "the walker, the innocent walker who does more than walk." I interpreted that as a warning that I might be mugged.

Newspaper headlines chronicled my route across the country:

LOIS DUNCAN WANTS TO GIVE HER DAUGHTER ONE FINAL GIFT—JUSTICE
New York Times

NON-FICTION MYSTERY IS RIVETING—
Connecticut Press

A MOTHER SEEKS HER CHILD'S KILLER—
Boston Globe

GRITTY SEARCH LEADS TO BOOK—
Bellingham Herald

The tour terminated in Los Angeles where I participated in a segment of *Sightings,* a Fox Network production that focused on paranormal happenings. Noreen Renier was filmed in her apartment in Florida, describing her psychic impressions of Kait's killer to a police artist, and Betty Muench was shown in her home in Albuquerque, taking dictation from her spirit guides. The major part of the reenactment was filmed in Albuquerque with the chase scene staged on Lomas Boulevard. Another scene was filmed at the cemetery with a photograph of Kait's face superimposed upon her grave stone.

At the LAX airport on my way back to Albuquerque, I picked up a paperback to read on the plane. Coincidentally the novel, *H Is for Homicide* by Sue Grafton, turned out to be about car wreck scams in Los Angeles. Among the resources listed on her acknowledgements page were Michael Fawcett, special agent for the National Insurance Crime Bureau, and Ron Wharthen, head of the fraud division of the California State Insurance Agencies.

The minute I got home, I contacted Sue, whom I once had met at a writers' conference, to get mailing addresses for Fawcett and Wharthen, and I sent them copies of my book.

Both men called to thank me.

"Your book lays out the case very well," Fawcett said. "We believe that some of the particular people you identify have been doing this type of crime for years."

Wharthen was equally supportive and went so far as to contact Bob Schwartz and request that he assign a researcher to the case. He also asked Schwartz to put pressure on the police to give us back the materials from Kait's desk, which they had been holding as evidence since August of 1989. Those items included a letter to Kait from the girlfriend of the capper, Bao Tran, and snapshots of other people in California, who we suspected might be participants in the insurance scam.

Prompted by Robin, I consulted two additional psychics. Robert Petro, a medium in Arizona, told me Kait's car had been stationery when she was shot and her killer looked familiar to her. Shelly Peck, a blind psychic in New York, described that killer, but her description didn't match that of either a Vietnamese man or Miguel Garcia, the Hispanic suspect charged with Kait's murder. She also made some confusing references to gas tanks.

In the time that I had been away, summer had crept from the Rio Grande Valley to the slopes of the Sandia Mountains, scattering wild flowers in its wake. I joined Don in our temporary trailer home and we tried to decide what to do next. Most people taking early retirement have already planned their next chapter of life, but for us that wasn't the case. We were running *away* from something, not running *to* something. So we procrastinated, clinging to the moment and allowing the beauty that surrounded us to become part of the storehouse of memories that we would carry with us.

In the evenings we sat outside on aluminum chairs, listening to the rhythmic chant of the cicadas and gazing up into the clearest skies in the world. At such times we reminisced about other summer evenings when we camped with our children at Elephant Butte Lake and, after gorging on hamburgers and toasted marshmallows, lay on blankets to watch for satellites passing overhead.

"What do you think will happen when we die?" Kait once asked me as she lay with her head on my shoulder, staring up into the depths of those enchanted purple skies. Not yet a prickly teenager, she was still ripe for cuddling. "Does our thinking part really go on in some other place?"

"Of course," I responded quickly. I wasn't all that sure about that, but I didn't want her to be afraid.

"I don't want my body to go to waste," Kait said. "I'm going to leave parts of it to people who aren't perfect like I am. Kerry can have my teeth. I bet she'll be happy to have a bunch of teeth with no fillings."

"I don't think I've ever heard of transplanting teeth," I told her, "but they do have a lot of success with things like kidneys. When the time comes for you to get your driver's license you can have them print on the back of it that you want to be an organ donor."

"I'll do that," Kait said solemnly. And then, with a shriek of excitement—"There's a falling star! Mother, quick, make a wish!"

What did I wish for on that long ago night of innocence and dreaming? I couldn't begin to remember. I wondered what Kait had wished for. I hoped it had not been a long term wish, but one that might actually have had a chance to come true in the limited time that was left to her before her heart and lungs went into the chest of a young optician from Santa Fe and her kidneys and liver were distributed to unidentified recipients.

Her set of perfect white teeth went into the grave with her.

So the long strange summer drifted past while Don and I remained cocooned in our artificial world of self-imposed tranquility, leaving camp only for occasional trips into town to buy groceries, pick up a newspaper, or check our voice mail.

On one such trip we opened the paper to learn that, two weeks earlier, Marty Martinez, the third of the men who were arrested, had phoned 911 to confess that he and his friends had been hired by the Vietnamese. He said that he personally had been paid one hundred dollars. Police had declined to interview him, and Marty's confession might have remained buried indefinitely if a reporter hadn't stumbled upon the 911 report. APD Lieutenant Chris Padilla then explained to reporters that police hadn't taken a statement because Marty had been drinking, and besides, they couldn't be sure that he really was one of the suspects who were arrested in 1990. He assured reporters that Marty would now be interviewed. Instead, the case was marked "Closed, Investigation Complete."

One newspaper article noted that "a connection to Asian crime gangs was a key element of Duncan's book, *Who Killed My Daughter?*, but investigators, including DA Bob Schwartz, have discounted it." That same night, the CBS Evening News ran a story about a crackdown on California car wreck scams. The California Insurance Commissioner told news anchor Connie Chung, "We have pierced the top echelon of a staged auto accident ring that has cost insurance companies tens of millions of dollars." A field reporter then stated, "Two books, including a best seller, have recently been written on the subject."

The camera panned to the jackets of *H Is for Homicide* and of my own book, holding steady on a close-up of Kait's smiling face.

We purchased a video of the show and sent it to Bob Schwartz. We also sent copies to the FBI in both Albuquerque and Los Angeles and to the producers of *Unsolved Mysteries*.

When Schwartz received his tape, he left a message on our voice mail.

"I've assigned an investigator to take another look at your

daughter's case," he told me when I returned his call. "My problem is that I have limited resources. I have only four investigators and their primary responsibility is to work on cases after the police have dropped them. It's very difficult to get a police officer to go back to a case after he's lost interest in it."

"I don't understand," I said. "I thought the DA had jurisdiction over the police."

"Only in the most theoretical of senses," Schwartz said. "According to the state constitution, the DA is the chief law enforcement officer for the district. I guarantee to you, however, that the day I start telling the police how to do things there are contracts that come in—the union comes in—the practical effect is they do not agree that I can do that."

"Kait's boyfriend told me he knew who killed Kait," I said. "As far as I know, no one has ever given him a high pressure interrogation."

"I agree with you, I think he should be interviewed hard," Schwartz said.

"Detective Gallegos could do it!" I suggested eagerly. "Dung seems to relate to him. Couldn't you use the good-cop-bad-cop thing they do on television and have Gallegos play the part of the good cop?"

"In order to do that you have to have a bad cop," Schwartz said. "That's where California comes into this. They do seem to have information about Dung's involvement in one car wreck—"

"In *two* car wrecks."

"All right, two car wrecks. But if the people in California choose not to prosecute, then he's not in trouble because it's a California crime. On the subject of Gallegos, I've asked him about the items you say were in Kait's desk."

"Why is APD keeping them?" I asked. "They've had them marked as evidence for over two years. How can they consider Kait's correspondence evidence of a 'random drive-by shooting'?"

"Gallegos says he doesn't have a record of those things," Schwartz said.

"He's told you he no longer has them?"

"No, he's not saying that exactly. He says he has no record of having seized them."

"There were a lot of snapshots in the sack we gave him!" I insisted. "Kait shot up two rolls of film on people in California."

"Gallegos says he doesn't have a record of any snapshots," Schwartz said. "I'm having difficulty being in the middle on this. You're indicating you gave APD certain items, and they're saying, 'We don't have them.'"

"Bob, why are they behaving like this?" I asked helplessly. "Why are they covering up for the Vietnamese?"

"I have absolutely no idea," Schwartz said. "I don't know. I mean, I don't think they are. The worst case scenario in my mind would be sloppy—unskilled—but certainly nothing intentional in covering for something else. Going beyond the point of negligence for me is—well, it's sort of my worst nightmare."

"You don't still think Kait's death was a random shooting, do you?" I asked him.

"That is still the scenario that has the most basis," Schwartz said. "A prosecutor's reality is defined not by truth but by evidence. Look, I'm sorry, but I've got a call on my other line."

Concerned that my grief-besotted memory might be playing tricks on me, I phoned Robin, who had helped me clear out Kait's apartment.

"Do you remember a bunch of photographs?" I asked her.

"Of course," Robin said immediately. "There were dozens of snapshots. A lot of them were of Kait and Dung, but others were of Dung's friends out in California."

"The insurance investigators need to have those pictures!" I exclaimed.

I wrote Bob Schwartz, telling him about the photographs and urging him to continue to try to get Steve Gallegos to release them. I also suggested that the DA's office seize Kait's apartment file.

"That file contains entries about Kait running to the manager in the night, asking for protection from the Vietnamese," I told him. "Wouldn't it be a good idea to confiscate that file before something happens to it?"

Schwartz didn't respond to my letter, but we later found out that he did belatedly have the police seize the apartment file and place it in evidence.

Soon after that we received letters from FBI agents in both Los Angeles and Albuquerque, politely acknowledging receipt of the information we had sent them. They said they had discussed our allegations with the Albuquerque Police Department, who did not feel that they warranted following up on.

The *Sightings* episode aired on the first of September 1992. The reenactment of the shooting was painful to watch, as it contained photographs that showed Kait's car with the driver's window shot out and a bullet hole in the door frame.

Although we didn't know it at the time, those photographs would turn out to be extremely meaningful.

Kait's car with bullet shattered window and bullet hole in door frame.

(Crime Scene photo)

CHAPTER FIVE

W hen the cottonwoods along the banks of the Rio Grande burst into gold, and patches of shimmering aspen dotted the mountains we realized that if we wanted to settle someplace before winter arrived we needed to get a move on.

Our younger son, Donnie, was the only one of our four surviving children still in Albuquerque. We tried to persuade him to come with us, but he refused to evacuate.

"This is my home," he said with characteristic stubbornness. "I'm not about to be forced out of it because my mom wrote a book that's got people pissed off."

The day before Don and I left we received a call from *Unsolved Mysteries* saying they were interested in doing a segment on Kait's murder but APD was not cooperating.

"We've tried everybody from the case detective to the chief of police," the researcher told me. "Nobody's willing to talk to us. We don't understand it. Police departments are usually eager to get their cases on our show because so many get solved that way. We need their assistance in getting background information and lining up people to interview."

I gave her contact information for Miguel Garcia's defense attorneys; for Mike Gallagher, the investigative reporter who had covered the case for the *Albuquerque Journal*; and for a number of

Kait's co-workers at the import store where Kait had been manager of imported clothing. I also suggested that, since Bob Schwartz had enjoyed his appearance on *Larry King Live,* he might be equally pleased to be on *Unsolved Mysteries.*

Our exodus from Albuquerque was stressful because we had no set destination. As we drove across beautiful countryside at the height of its autumn glory, one of us would occasionally comment, "This seems like a nice town. Do you want to live here?" and the other would say, "Let's keep going and see what's ahead." We continued to drive until the road ran out on the Outer Banks of North Carolina. The smell of salt air brought back memories of my childhood in Florida, and my heart lifted. Don, too, was caught by the magic of windswept beaches and endless stretches of ocean, so different from his own background as a Michigan farm boy. With little discussion we rented a house in the dunes.

Meanwhile the *Unsolved Mysteries* show was solidifying even without the help of law enforcement. The producer requested pictures of our family to aid them in selecting actors for the reenactment. With the thought that a video would be more helpful to them than still pictures, Don unpacked the box of home videos that we had carted with us across the country. We were stunned to discover that all the tapes with Kait on them were missing. The commercial videos were there, and the tapes of our grandchildren, but every one of our family videos of Christmases, birthdays, campouts and ski vacations had vanished.

We phoned our children to see if one of them might have borrowed them, perhaps when they were home for the funeral. All said they hadn't.

"They were there that first Christmas after the shooting," Robin told us. "I know because I started to watch one. It was the one with Kait at the lake showing off her new swimsuit, and Dung and his friends were cavorting on an inflatable raft. I looked at Kait, so young and dumb and unsuspecting, and I wanted to scream at her, 'Run! Get away from those people!' I couldn't stand to watch it all the way through. I rewound it and put it back on the shelf with the others."

"Then they must have disappeared at some point between Christmas of 1989 and March 1990," Don said. "March is when we boxed up our stuff and put the house up for sale."

"But that's not when we moved out," I reminded him. "The Hispanics were arrested in January. That's when we got death threats and I panicked. We lived in a studio apartment for a month before we rented the town house and put our things in storage. So there was a period of time when our house was unoccupied with all our possessions still in it."

"There weren't any signs of a break-in."

"If somebody had a key—"

"Nobody had a key to our home except our kids."

We finally decided that some of the videos must have been packed in a box that was lost during our move. How ironic and heartbreaking that those were the videos that showed Kait!

We provided *Unsolved Mysteries* with snapshots from our photo albums, and I made a trip back to Albuquerque to be interviewed for the show along with reporter, Mike Gallagher, and case detective, Steve Gallegos. The producer told me Bob Schwartz and the APD captain who had appeared on *Good Morning, America* initially had agreed to be interviewed, but both canceled out at the last minute, and Detective Gallegos was reluctantly thrust into that slot.

Casting the part of Dung had turned out to be a problem.

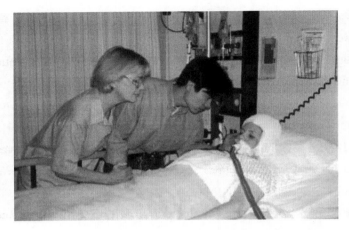

Unsolved Mysteries' reenactment of the death scene.
(Photo by Lois Duncan)

There had been no difficulty finding Albuquerque actors to portray members of our family but no one wanted to play the part of Kait's boyfriend.

"It's crazy," the producer told me. "There are lots of Vietnamese registered with Albuquerque talent agencies and when we posted an announcement that we needed Asian actors they were beating down the doors to get parts. That was before word got out that it was the Kait Arquette story. After that, not one Vietnamese actor would audition."

They ended up importing an actor from Hollywood.

Donnie went with me to watch the filming of the death scene. In a bizarre trip back through time, actors and actresses who bore an eerie resemblance to our family gathered around a hospital bed where a young actress who looked a lot like Kait lay with her head encased in bandages. The line on the monitor blipped up and down erratically as it had on the night when the girl on the bed had been our own.

56

Donnie's hand tightened around mine until I thought my fingers would snap.

"It wasn't the car-wrecks," he muttered. "It was something much bigger."

"I think so too," I responded.

When I got back to North Carolina, Don told me we'd had a phone call from an insurance claims investigator in California named Jim Ellis.

"He asked that you call him as soon as you got back," Don said.

Jim came onto the line with a burst of such high level energy that the receiver seemed to vibrate in my hand.

"When I saw you on *Sightings*, I rushed out to buy your book," he said. "Then I went straight to my computer and started pulling up the claims that have come out of Albuquerque involving accidents in Southern California. The number was staggering, and the same addresses and phone numbers kept coming up over and over. A couple of the addresses are on a bunch of different policies—one on Texas Street and the other on Kathryn Street." He told me the street numbers. "Does either of those sound familiar?"

"Both Dung Nguyen and An Quoc Le once lived at the Kathryn Street address," I said.

"Well, it looks like they've got a bunch of friends living there too, who are playing the same game they are," Jim said. "And that Texas Street address appears on even more claims. The most recent loss from that address occurred in July of this year. A guy named Vu Nguyen was killed."

"Have you found any cases involving Dung and his friends?" I asked him.

"Possibly," Jim said. "That dead guy's roommate, Ngoc Nguyen, was involved in a wreck in Santa Ana on March 24, 1989. That's the same week Dung and Kait were out there. In Ngoc's wreck, an auto body shop with a questionable reputation declared his car a total loss. All occupants of the other car were represented by the law firm of Minh Nguyen Duy, the attorney whose law firm's name was on Bao Tran's business card."

"Dung had a friend named Ngoc Nguyen," I said. "His name was on Kait's speed dial. Is there any way to determine if he was that person?"

"Only by Social Security number," Jim said. "These people often have identical names, and the crooks mix and match their addresses. Today, for example, I brought up a case on the computer where a person bought a policy in Albuquerque, rushed to California, had an accident, and gave a home address in Garden Grove."

"Why haven't those people been arrested?" I asked.

"Insurance companies aren't interested in the little fish," Jim said. "They want the people at the top. Very soon now there's going to be a bust that will bring down a bunch of attorneys and clinics and doctors. In the process maybe somebody will know something about this New Mexico ring and we can work off of that. Where's Bao Tran right now?"

"I don't know," I said. "I have his address in Santa Ana, but it's possible he's moved, because his phone and beeper numbers have been disconnected."

"I'll keep on pulling up cases and maybe Tran's name will pop out," Jim said. "For whatever reason, APD seems to have stonewalled this whole thing. The good news is that the DA in Albuquerque has reopened the investigation."

"We're afraid that may be a token gesture," I said.

"I'm not going to allow that," Jim assured me. "That's why I'm trying to get together as much evidence as I can. I want to get the National Insurance Crime Bureau, the Fraud Division of the California State Insurance Agencies, and representatives from all the insurance carriers all working together so the list we compile will be so overwhelming that DA Schwartz will be forced to take it seriously."

The kindness in his voice was almost more than I could handle.

"Thank you," I said, fighting back tears of gratitude.

"I know this is hard for you to believe, Lois, but in the long run the Universe is perfect," Jim said gently. "It was no accident that I happened to see that *Sightings* show. You and I are both part of a plan that's unfolding as it's meant to. We're going to put a bunch of crooks behind bars, and we're going to find out what happened to your daughter."

Jim's first move was to start weaving together an extensive network of interrelated car wrecks stemming from names in my book. When I mailed him a copy of the accident report on Dung's wreck in August 1988, he discovered that the second vehicle in the wreck was registered to Bao Tran's girlfriend. He then ran the names of the claimants through his computer and discovered that one of them, a man from Garden Grove, had been a driver in a similar wreck in October 1991.

"This looks like a hit!" he announced with satisfaction. "I've had my eye on this guy. I already had him under investigation by a private investigator."

A second party who claimed injuries in Dung's 1988 wreck was convicted arsonist, Hong Phuc Duy Van, in whose name Bao Tran's home phone had been registered.

Jim sent me manila envelopes crammed with reports of suspicious accidents, and I entered the names and addresses into my own database. Eventually I reached a point where certain addresses and phone numbers became red flags that allowed me to pinpoint possible fraudulent claims before even reading the reports.

The *Unsolved Mysteries* segment on Kait's case aired early in 1993. In light of our strained relationship with APD, the producer sent us our own copies of the tips that were called in to their 800 number. Most were about insurance scams in California, and those I forwarded to Jim.

But one that *Unsolved Mysteries* classified as a "Hot Tip" was from Susan Smith, who told the hot line operator that she wanted to correct an inaccuracy in my book.

She said she was living in fear and wanted her phone number given only to me.

When I dialed the number a woman's voice answered.

"Hello, Susan?" I said.

There was no response, so after a moment I tried again.

"Am I talking to Susan? This is Lois Arquette, Kait's mother."

"Oh, it's you!" the woman said shakily. "You took me by surprise. I don't go by Susan anymore."

"The people at *Unsolved Mysteries* said you wanted me to call you."

"Yes, that's right," Susan said. "I wanted to correct something. In your book you said Kait got to my house at nine-thirty. That's not right. She got there much earlier than that."

"The police report quotes you as saying she got there at nine-thirty."

"She got there at seven," Susan said. "I'd invited her for seven-thirty but she got there early. She came straight from seeing *Working Girl*. That movie let out at seven, and since the theater was right near my house, she thought it didn't make sense for her to go home and come all the way back, so she just came on over."

"Kait wasn't at a movie!" I said.

"*Working Girl*. She said it was really good."

"Susan, she couldn't have gone to a movie," I said. "She left our house at six-fifteen, saying she was going to your house for six-thirty dinner. There's no way she could have seen a movie between six-fifteen and seven o'clock."

"All I know is that's what she told me," Susan insisted. "She told me she came straight from the movie *Working Girl*, and she saw it at the Lobo Theater, and it was a dollar movie, and she was telling me about how good it was. And the reason I know she got there not late in the evening is that it was still light out."

"This is very confusing," I said.

"She was acting flaky," Susan said. "She wasn't like herself at all. She'd be crying, and then she'd be laughing, and then she'd start crying again, and then she'd have me on a mission calling Dung over and over to see if he was home. And then she started telling me about the insurance scams. That really surprised me because I didn't think Kait would be involved in anything like that. I guess in my own mind I had her like a Goody Two Shoes. So, then, you know, I've kept thinking, why did she tell me that night, when she'd certainly had other opportunities?"

"Why do you think?" I asked.

"I think the chips were down, personally," Susan said. "I think that she knew something was about to happen and—"

LOIS DUNCAN

"Think really hard," I broke in. "What might she have said that makes you think she knew something was going to happen? The car wreck she witnessed occurred four months earlier. Why do you think *that night* she was spilling this out and frightened?"

"I don't know," Susan said. "She was just so anxious that night. Like I said, she had me dialing Dung over and over. I was just sitting there hitting redial."

"You don't feel she was calling to patch things up?"

"No way!" Susan said adamantly. "She didn't want to talk to him; she just wanted to know where he was. She said if he answered I should hang up like it was a wrong number. And when it got to be ten forty-five and he still didn't answer, she suddenly said, 'I'm really sorry, but we'll do this another night, because I just remembered that I have a test I have to take in the morning. I've got to go home and study.'"

"But you told the police Kait spent the afternoon studying at the library!"

"I never said that," Susan said.

"It's in the police report."

"Detective Gallegos wrote down everything wrong. Kait never said anything about studying at the library. And she didn't get to my house at nine-thirty, it was seven. And there's another thing that's been getting under my skin. When Kait was in a coma and I came to the hospital, Dung told me, 'This is all my fault.' I have a very strong feeling Kait's shooting was not a random drive-by. I think it had something to do with Dung and his friends and the stuff they were into."

"Have you ever been threatened?" I asked her.

There was a long pause.

62

Then she said, "No."

"Then why did you leave Albuquerque?"

"I'm nervous when I'm in Albuquerque," Susan said. "I didn't tell anyone but one friend where I moved to, and she was sworn to ultimate secrecy. I had to send away for my income tax statements, and I had them sent to her address. I was motivated to call *Unsolved Mysteries* because I could tell that different things had gotten lost in the cracks, but I was really scared. When I answered the phone and you said 'Susan,' my blood ran cold. My mom still calls me Susan, of course, but she's the only one."

By the end of that conversation, I was so confused that I felt I had entered the Twilight Zone. Was it possible that Detective Gallegos had misquoted almost everything Susan said? If ever there was one interview that he should have recorded correctly you would have expected it to have been that one. Susan was the first person he interviewed and the last person to talk to Kait before she was shot.

An alternate possibility was that Gallegos's report was accurate and it was Susan who was lying. Might she initially have told him the truth and now be attempting to replace that with a fabrication? Why had Susan invented the scenario about a movie? And why had she considered it so imperative to convince us that there were no missing hours in Kait's final evening that she'd had a man—who, Don suspected, might have been a cop—track Don down at a secluded campground to deliver that message? And now, over a year later, she had contacted me through a TV hot line to reiterate the same story, this time adding the embellishment of a movie. What had happened to Kait during the early part of that evening that Susan might not have wanted known?

With my mind too filled with Kait's case to be able to focus on writing books, my main activity during our first winter in North Carolina was responding to reader mail. Those letters gave me a disconcerting sense of deja vu. Back in 1984, I had written a novel called *The Third Eye,* in which I described how a teenage psychic was bombarded with letters from parents of murdered and missing children:

> *"Each afternoon when Karen arrived home from school she was greeted by a mailbox filled with desperation," I had written. "She could almost feel the agony of the contents burning her hands when she handled the unopened envelopes."*

Now it was my own mailbox that erupted with such agony:

> *"My daughter's body was found May 29, 1992. The police said her death was a suicide but there are things that don't fit. Why would she have gone to the door to kill herself? And why would the gun have been in her right hand when the bullet entered the left side of her head?"*

> *"We too lost our daughter. A neighbor said he heard a woman screaming 'Mom!' in the orchard behind our home . . . There lay my beautiful girl with a gunshot wound to the head. I began running right through a barbed wire fence . . . We were told she committed suicide, but things look awfully suspicious. We've found out she had just turned in her first husband for drug trafficking. There are three different detectives that wrote three conflicting reports on her death. They didn't even have the right day."*

> *"My husband and I lost our daughter in Massachusetts. The police*

closed the case as a suicide by hanging, but a forensic expert told us he thinks Valarie was strangled and then strung up. She had just put out a restraining order against her boyfriend, saying, 'He took his gun out and threatened to shoot me ... He's also threatened to cut up my face, set me on fire, kill me while I sleep, and chop up my dog. I am in fear of my life. He has threatened to use all his police powers to destroy me if I ever try to leave him.' Her boyfriend was a member of the police department. Valarie was found strung up in his cellar."

I responded to every letter but could offer no comfort or solutions, for these parents were asking the same questions we were: What had gone wrong with the System?

CHAPTER SIX

The Los Angeles Times, January 14, 1993

DOZENS HELD IN MASSIVE INSURANCE SCAM

Ending an 18-month investigation targeted at attorneys and doctors charged with cheating insurance companies out of millions of dollars, authorities have arrested at least 35 people in Orange and San Diego counties suspected of running one of the biggest auto insurance fraud schemes in state history.

More than 150 federal, state and local law enforcement officers swarmed the two counties, arresting suspects indicted for their roles in four loosely connected fraud rings that bilked insurance companies with phony auto accident claims.

Investigators say unscrupulous lawyers operate offices in Little Saigon staffed by Vietnamese legal assistants who are actually "cappers," people who sell accident cases to lawyers in violation of state law. The "cappers," some of whom are gang members, receive as much as $1,500 a head and can earn more than $150,000 a year by soliciting two or three cases a week.

The record setting crackdown that Jim Ellis had predicted led to over forty arrests with an additional seventy suspects still under investigation. Most of those arrested were doctors and lawyers in

Orange County, and several of the Vietnamese car wreck "victims" were from Albuquerque.

Jim continued to phone almost daily to fill us in on what was happening.

"We've latched onto a huge network," he reported. "There's one guy who gave a Westminster address on a police report, but I recognized the phone number, and further research showed that he had the same address as Bao Tran. There's another guy, Suu Dinh, that we also know lived there. I recognize him from a loss back in 1990 in which there was a connection with a guy named Duc Dat Tran. Duc Dat Tran was using Bao Tran's address in June 1991, when he was hit by a stolen vehicle."

"You've turned up so much!" I exclaimed.

"It doesn't stop with me, Lois," Jim said. "Whenever I'm helping another carrier, I just casually mention your case and—boom!— they're caught up in it too. Last week, I was contacted by an attorney named Michael Bush who has a case going that coincides with a case of mine. He bought thirty copies of your book and has been distributing them everywhere. He even gave one to the Orange County District Attorney."

"Do you think these fraud cases are the reason for Kait's murder?" I asked him. "Psychics say Kait found out about a drug operation."

"I don't doubt that at all," Jim said. "Such crooks aren't one dimensional. Many of those same people import drugs from the Orient. High purity white heroin from Asia is worth much more than black tar heroin from Mexico. The thing is, we have the equipment to track down the car scams, but not the drug smuggling. So this is the path we have to follow."

Asian heroin.

Soon after that Jim phoned to tell me that they'd found Bao Tran.

"You're not going to believe this," he said. "On a whim, Michael Bush decided to dial one of the numbers you found on Kait's final phone bill. It was *good!* Bao Tran *called him back!*"

"Tran reinstated his phone numbers?"

"I guess he must have," Jim said. "Anyway, not knowing who'd called him or what they wanted, he returned Michael's call. Tran said all the things you accused him of are lies."

"I only reported what Dung told the police," I said.

"Dung is Tran's least favorite person in the world, next to you," Jim said. "He said the calls from Kait's apartment couldn't have been made to him because he was in Vietnam."

"Can he prove that by showing his passport?"

"He says Dung's alibi witness, An Quoc Le, has forbidden that. An Le is back in Albuquerque at that communal address on Kathryn Street they all keep using and seems to be controlling things from there."

"Did Tran say where Dung is?"

"Tran said the last he'd heard of him he was in the Pacific Northwest with some Caucasian girl. That's where they seem to be going now. A lot of the guys who were staging accidents in California are now in Portland."

"Is there any way to force Bao Tran to give a statement?"

"If we can get the DA in Albuquerque to cooperate with the DA in Orange County we might be able to," Jim said. "According to protocol, the Orange DA has to receive a request from the DA in Albuquerque before he can do anything."

"So all it will take to get Bao Tran deposed is a request from Bob Schwartz?"

"That's right," Jim said. "And it's the only way to make Tran talk. Michael's volunteered to take on the job of convincing Schwartz since I've become unpopular at the DA's office. The last time I talked to their investigator I lost my temper and told her I think it's criminal the way this case has been mishandled. That didn't go down well, since her husband is a captain with APD. I've sent them boxes of information about this fraud ring and there's no indication that anyone has followed up on any of it."

On the heels of Jim's call, I received a call from Michael Bush.

"This case draws me like a magnet," he told me. "When I read your book I recognized the lawyer Minh Nguyen Duy. He and I were currently involved in litigation. I want to go to Albuquerque and

69

meet with the D.A. there. He's got to be made to understand what it is we're dealing with."

"What will you charge us for doing that?" I asked him. Now that Don was retired and I no longer was churning out suspense novels our income had dropped significantly.

"No charge," Michael said. "What I'm striving for is pure motives. Once you start doing something for compensation, even expenses, things get fuzzy. What if I turn up evidence of something you don't agree with? I don't want you and your family to be in a position to tell me not to expose that. I just want to see if I can help you get to the truth."

When I repeated that conversation to Don, he shook his head in disbelief.

"When something seems too good to be true, there's usually a catch," he said. "Why don't we see what Betty Muench has to say about this?"

Betty's reading came back by return mail:

QUESTION: WHAT MAY I KNOW ABOUT MICHAEL BUSH AND ABOUT HIS ROLE IN SOLVING THE MYSTERY OF KAIT'S MURDER?

ANSWER: There is in Michael this energy which will have had him in a distant time—a past life—involved with those of this family who will be now unaware of how they will move. Michael will have been one to come along behind this family of warriors and take tally. His tally will sometimes have caused him great alarm at the power of this group. All in this family will have known Michael Bush as the Tally Keeper, and there will be now the consulting in order to have him continue to keep track of these past life soldiers, these warriors, who will be now led in one direction, and this is this mystery of the loss of one of their own.

Kait will remember Michael as one who picked her up before out of the devastation and carried her to safety and continued life. It is as if he cannot accept that she will have now been lost in the war in this lifetime, one in which he was not there to carry her back to the fort to safety. This time it is all on a less tangible level but he will want this work and this lesson and this opportunity to assist again.

Michael timed his trip to Albuquerque to coincide with my speaking engagement at a writers' conference. When we met for breakfast it was as if I had known him forever.

"The fraud ring is the tip of the iceberg," he told me. "It's a lever we can use to get law enforcement to take this case seriously, but Jim and I are agreed that Kait was killed for some other reason— probably

Michael Bush, Lois Duncan and Jim Ellis. *(Courtesy: Don Arquette)*

drugs."

"Everyone who knew Kait has told us she didn't use drugs."

"That's what would have made her a threat to smugglers," Michael said. "If she wasn't part of the game, she'd be a danger to the players."

He proceeded to give me a rundown on his activities since his arrival in Albuquerque the previous day.

"Schwartz refused to meet with me," he said. "But the reporter, Mike Gallagher, did. Did you know the police found a Budweiser can on the curb across from where Kait was shot?"

"There was something about that in the case file, but it didn't seem important," I said. "The autopsy didn't show any alcohol in Kait's blood."

"The significant thing is that there was a viable fingerprint on that can," Michael said. "We need to get prints of the Vietnamese suspects from Immigration so APD can do a comparison."

"Another thing Gallagher told me was that a truck driver reported seeing a high speed chase involving a car like Kait's and a low rider Camaro like Juve's. But that chase occurred around nine thirty, over an hour before Kait left Susan's house."

"We suspect that Kait may have been on her way *to* Susan's house at that time," I said. "The truck driver said the cars were headed west in the direction of Susan's place, not east in the direction Kait was driving when she was shot. Susan now denies this, but Detective Gallegos quoted her as saying Kait got to her house at nine-thirty."

"That would mean Kait was chased twice that night," Michael said, "once on her way to her friend's house and once when she left. What reason did Susan give for changing her story about Kait's arrival time?"

"She said Detective Gallegos misquoted her."

"That's unlikely but not impossible," Michael said. "What was Susan's demeanor at the funeral?"

"She didn't attend it," I said. "Her dog bit her, and she was in the emergency room getting her arm stitched up."

"She was bitten *by her own dog?*"

"That's what she said."

"And that was on the day of Kait's funeral? Isn't that the same date Dung Nguyen tried to kill himself?"

"Mike Gallagher doesn't buy that," I said. "He thinks Dung was stabbed as a warning to keep his mouth shut."

"If that's so, that same person may have gotten to Susan," Michael speculated. "I'd like to talk to that woman. Do you know how to reach her?"

"Yes, but I told her I'd keep her location confidential."

"Then give her my number and ask her to call me," Michael said. "My guess is that Susan may know a lot more than she's told people."

As soon as I got back to my room I dialed Susan's number and left that message on her answering machine.

From then on, every time I came back to my room between workshop sessions, the light on my phone was blinking with a new message from Michael:

1:10 p.m.: "I've talked to a Vietnamese guy who was a friend of Kait's. He says he has information but won't divulge it unless he's guaranteed protection."

3:07 p.m.: "I'm calling from the office of Miguel Garcia's defense attorney. He's got copies of some of Detective Gallegos's field notes, and one of them says Kait's next door neighbor saw her followed from her apartment by a VW Bug."

5:42 p.m.: "I've met with the new manager of Kait's apartment complex. He said last week a young blonde woman came in pretending to want an apartment. She said she'd been a friend of Kait's and started asking the manager a lot of questions about Dung. It finally came out that she hadn't known Kait at all. She was Dung's new girlfriend from Oregon. Dung's moved back to Albuquerque and brought her with him, and she's apparently heard enough rumors so she's checking up on him."

The luncheon on Saturday was a highlight of the writers' conference. As we neared the end of the main course a woman across from me suddenly exclaimed, "Aren't those pretty!" I turned in my chair to see a young man headed in our direction with an elaborate arrangement of silk flowers. People were craning their necks to follow his progress as he worked his way across the room, struggling to avoid colliding with tray-laden wait people.

Assuming the floral arrangement was for the luncheon speaker, I resumed my conversation with the person next to me. Then, to my astonishment, the flowers were plunked down in front of me.

The conversation at our table was extinguished in a heartbeat. Everybody stared at me expectantly as I removed the card from its envelope. The message on it was the last I would ever have expected.

Mrs. Arquette, I wish you the best in finding Kait's killer. I don't think I have the answers you seek, but someday I would like to meet you. You're a strong mother and I wish Kait had introduced us before she left. I hope this arrangement shows that there are some out here who are still looking and love her very much. Rod.

I felt as if somebody had crashed a fist into my chest. According to psychics, Rod was Kait's secret second boyfriend. For four years I had been searching for evidence that this man existed, and now suddenly, here he was!

Our lunch plates had by now been removed from the table and a glass of tangerine sherbet of the exact same shade as the flowers sat melting in front of me. Somebody at the head table was clinking a spoon against a glass to indicate the start of the program. Mumbling an awkward apology to my tablemates, I picked up the flower arrangement and carried it out to the lobby.

"Do you know who delivered these?" I asked the clerk at the front desk.

He said he did not.

I went up to my room and set the arrangement on the table next to the bed. It was exceptionally pretty and clearly not inexpensive. There was even a little feathered bird nestled among the clusters of pastel blossoms.

I wondered if it had a bomb in it.

How in God's name could I know the intentions of the sender? Who was this "Rod" and how did he fit into the picture? Was this the young man who allegedly took Kait to a party at a "Desert Castle" where she saw a VIP involved in a drug transaction?

The phone rang.

I snatched up the receiver, but it was only Michael checking in with the news of the day.

"So what's going on at the conference?" he asked conversationally.

"Rod sent me flowers," I told him.

"The kid you described in your book? He's finally revealed himself?"

"Not exactly," I said. I read him the message on the card. "He doesn't give his last name or say how to contact him."

"What was the name of the flower shop?" Michael asked. "I'll check and see if they remember the order." A short time later he called back to report that the proprietors had no trouble recalling the flower arrangement because they knew the young man who bought it.

"They don't know his name, but every Friday since Kait's death he's come in to buy flowers to take to her grave," Michael said. "It's gone on so long that he just asks for 'the usual.' Next Friday I'm going to fly back here and try to intercept him.

"Oh, and guess what? Susan left me a message on my voice mail. She won't give me her home address, but she told me what city she's living in and has agreed to meet me at a coffee shop in a shopping mall. I've made plane reservations for this evening."

"You're going to fly there!" I exclaimed. "This has to be costing you a fortune! Couldn't you just ask her questions over the phone?"

"I want to get a look at that dog bite scar," Michael told me.

CHAPTER SEVEN

Michael sent us a tape of his interview with Susan and then phoned to discuss it.

"She was pretty convincing," he said. "But her statements conflict with each other. She told you that she left Albuquerque because she was scared. She told *me* she relocated because of a wonderful job offer."

"What was your impression of the scar on her arm?" I asked him.

"It's a straight slash about four inches long, and I didn't see any opposing set of tooth marks. Susan says it tore a bunch of tendons and required three hours of surgery, which seems like a lot of damage for a nip from your own dog.[1] She told me, 'The scar looks weird because it got stitched funny.' I asked if she'd be willing to let us look at the ER report. She insisted she has nothing to hide, so I've mailed her release forms. It's important to nail this down because an amazing number of people suffered suspicious injuries following Kait's murder."

"Dung's suicide attempt—"

"It goes far beyond that. Dung's Hispanic friend, Ray Padilla, and two of Ray's woman friends had their arms and wrists slashed. Ray's the guy who told police that Dung had friends in California who were big time drug dealers. When your book came out, Marty

Martinez was found lying in his doorway with his wrist slashed, an alleged suicide attempt. And after Miguel Garcia got out of jail, he was shot in the stomach, another alleged suicide attempt. And Robert Garcia, APD's false eyewitness, was found dead in an alley. That adds up to a lot of injuries to people linked in one way or another to Kait's case."

Susan did not sign the forms to release her ER records. She told Michael she hadn't received them. He mailed her a second set, which she didn't sign either. After that she screened all her calls and would not respond to those from Michael.

I wrote to her, pleading with her to sign the forms so we could get that issue off our platter. "The doctor's description of your wound should clearly indicate that it's a dog bite, and that will be that," I wrote.

She did not respond.

True to his word, Michael flew back to Albuquerque to hang out at the flower shop and wait for the mysterious "Rod" to show up the next Friday. Rod came into the shop right on schedule, and Michael intercepted him.

"Rod and Kait went to high school together," Michael reported. "He has an I.D. bracelet she gave him for his birthday. He had to change schools and the two lost track of each other, but he ran into her again in 1989 and they started going out for coffee or to a movie on nights when Dung was off with his buddies. Rod says Kait was close-mouthed about what was going on in her life. He says he didn't know anything about the car wrecks until he read about them in your book. And he swears he didn't take her to the Desert Castle.

"Two days before the shooting, Kait asked him, 'What would you do if I died?' He thought she was joking.[2] Then, she did die, and

he's been going through hell ever since. It sounds like she was prim-
ing herself to confide in him, and he didn't take her seriously. We
definitely need to find out if the print on that Budweiser can belongs
to one of the Vietnamese suspects."

I phoned the Immigration and Naturalization Service office in
Albuquerque and requested that they provide APD with the immigration files for Dung and his alibi friends. I spoke with an agent
named Doug[3] who was extremely sympathetic because his daughter
had gone to school with Kait and because his friend, Police Chief
Sam Baca, had told him Kait was killed by the Vietnamese. Spurred
by that disclosure, Doug had ordered the immigration files for Dung
and his friends sent up from the regional office in El Paso. When he
attempted to give them to the APD, the police had not wanted them,
so he had sent them back to Texas.

I asked him, please, to get them back and check to see if they
contained any information that might help us.

He did so and phoned me, sounding very excited.

"There's something crazy going on!" he said. "An Quoc Le has
a double!"

"A double?" I repeated blankly.

"In 1987, an An Quoc Le who lived in Westminster was naturalized in California. A person with a different face, but with the same
name and same date of birth, was naturalized in Albuquerque in
1991. I'm not sure yet which is the legally naturalized An Quoc Le.
I'll have to compare the fingerprints."

"An Quoc Le is a common Vietnamese name," I said. "Couldn't
this be a coincidence?"

"No," Doug said with certainty. "One of these guys is an

impostor. The An Quoc Le who came to Albuquerque was admitted to the United States in 1982. An Quoc Le Number Two, the one in California, was naturalized in 1987, using the same Alien Registration Number."

I gave him the Social Security number for "our" An Quoc Le.

"That matches the one who was naturalized in Albuquerque," Doug said. "We've definitely got two individuals. Hopefully when we get through investigating we'll denaturalize one of them. When I find out more, I'll let you know."

Day after day we waited for him to call back, but, like other good men before him, he seemed to have been road-blocked. An Quoc Le continued to enjoy the lifestyle to which he had become accustomed, and we were never to hear from that nice INS agent again.

However, something did soon come out of Albuquerque to give new direction to our thinking.

"Does the name Matt Griffin mean anything to you?" Michael asked me.

"Wasn't he the cop who was the 'Ninja Bandit'?"

"That's the one," Michael said. "The press started calling him the Ninja because he dressed all in black and leapt over counters during bank robberies. His get-away cars were stolen sports cars. He's currently serving a life sentence for shooting a witness."

"I remember that," I said. "He was arrested the same week Kait was shot."

"That story is back in the news again," Michael said. "In January 1989, Griffin killed a man named Peter Klunck. The official story was that it was self-defense. Well, it's now come to light that the APD Internal Affairs files contain information that Peter was

GRIFFIN: No contact with other prisoners

Matt Griffin, the Ninja Bandit. *(Courtesy: Albuquerque Journal)*

once Griffin's snitch. There's also a rumor that Griffin's fellow officers covered up for him."

"What does this have to do with Kait?" I asked him.

"The federal prosecutors have demanded to examine the I.A. reports. APD refuses to release them."

"But what's the connection—"

"I'm getting to that," Michael said. "A P.I. in Albuquerque,

Roy Nolan*, has been investigating an auto repair shop that's an alleged chop shop for stolen cars. A cop friend of Nolan's told him that one of the I.A. reports contains information that Vietnamese were stealing getaway cars for Griffin, which were later dismantled at that shop. That isn't as crazy as it sounds, because one way the fraud rings operate is by stealing cars to use to stage hit and run accidents.

"If it's true that members of Dung's bunch were working for Griffin, then it's likely they have inside knowledge about the Klunck shooting. If that includes the fact that cops planted an alibi gun at the scene, it would put that group in a position to blackmail those cops."

"Can APD be forced to release the Internal Affairs files?"

"A judge has ruled that they must, but they continue to refuse to," Michael told me. "My guess is they plan to hold out until it's too late to prosecute. The statute of limitations on criminal prosecution runs out on January 27."

In February, Don and I made a trip to Albuquerque to visit Donnie. While there, we went to the library to see what we could find out about Matt Griffin.

We started by pulling up articles from the time of the Klunck shooting. According to the *Albuquerque Journal,* police Chief Sam Baca told reporters that Peter was shot twice in the chest—*when in reality he was shot three times in the back.* The *Journal* also had somehow obtained a confidential report that disclosed that the three officers who fired at Peter gave conflicting statements. Matt Griffin, whose bullet was defined as the one that killed Peter, refused to give a statement at the scene. Officer Robert Valtierra said Peter had a gun in his *left* hand. Sergeant Paul Heatley said he clearly saw a gun

Renee Klunck and Lois Duncan. *(Courtesy: Dick Klunck)*

in Peter's *right* hand. Officer Steve Nakamura, who did not fire at Peter, reported that Peter was unarmed.

The gun that Peter allegedly had been carrying was not found until seven hours later when a derringer turned up fifteen feet from where Peter fell. It tested negative for prints.

Griffin then gave a statement that he had fired in self-defense.

The grand jury, who weren't aware of the conflicting statements of the police officers, found them not criminally liable, although they did raise questions about the delayed appearance of the derringer. Peter Klunck's parents had questions about that too, and in January 1990, they filed a federal wrongful death and civil rights suit against the police chief and several officers. The city settled out of court for $325,000, which the Kluncks placed in trust for Peter's son, born twenty days after his death. The settlement contained no admission that Peter's civil rights were violated.

The Klunck family refused to give up on the civil rights issue and contacted the FBI in Washington D.C. In December 1993, a federal grand jury subpoenaed APD's Internal Affairs files, which APD still refused to release.

An editorial in the January 10, 1994, issue of the *Albuquerque Journal* gave an update on the case:

"Five years later, Klunck's death is still haunted by troubling questions ... Now thanks to investigations by federal prosecutors, a startling possible link between Klunck and the officer who fired the fatal shot— Matt Griffin—has been included for the first time in public records. Prosecutors say they have developed evidence that Klunck and Griffin were engaged in criminal activity together and Klunck was in the process of making the officer's criminal activity known on the day he was killed ... Could a policeman who had possible criminal links with Klunck have a compelling personal reason to want to silence Klunck— a personal motive for firing bullets into the man's back?"

I phoned Peter's mother, Renee Klunck, and asked if she would talk with me. She said to come right over and the moment we met we bonded into instant sisterhood.

"When I read your book, I went out of my tree!" Renee told me.

"I sat there, pounding my fists on the kitchen counter as I read the names of the very same cops who dealt with us.

"Our son had a drug problem, and Griffin was part of it. A police officer told the FBI that Griffin had Pete pushing speed for him. Then, in October 1988, Griffin ordered Peter to steal a car for him, but this time Peter turned him down. Pete's girlfriend was expecting a baby, and he was getting into rehab and trying to turn his life around.

"On the day of his death, Pete was scheduled for an appearance in court, and he told me he was going to blow the lid off APD. But it was more than just squealing on Griffin. Pete had the goods on VIPs who control the New Mexico drug scene. That morning he called his girlfriend and told her he loved her and if anything happened to him he wanted her to keep the baby."

"What do *you* think happened that morning?" I asked her.

"According to the Internal Affairs file, Officer Nakamura—the honest cop—had Peter out of the car with both hands in the air and no gun in either one of them, when they heard a gunshot. Peter looked behind him and took off running. My guess is he may have seen Griffin running toward him and realized he was going to be killed."

"How can you possibly know what's in the Internal Affairs file?"

"I stole it," Renee said.

I stared at her in amazement.

"You *stole* the Internal Affairs file?"

"I prefer to consider it 'borrowing,'" Renee said mildly. "I was in an attorney's office, sort of poking around while the lawyer was in the john, and right there on his desk was that file. I read it, of course, and when I came to the part where Officer Nakamura told his supervisor, 'I can't believe it! *They shot him in the back and he didn't even have a gun!'* I flipped! Nakamura also said Peter followed all instructions and made no threatening gestures, and two other officers backed him up on that. I knew nobody would believe me if I quoted that statement, so I tucked the file under my arm, walked out past the secretary, and got the thing copied. Then I sneaked the original back before it was missed."

"My God!" I exclaimed in awe. "How wonderful!"

"I only did what I had to do," Renee said modestly. "There's so much evidence of a police cover-up you wouldn't believe it. Rheardon's report—he's the former chief justice who investigated for the police department—says in his very first paragraph, 'I believe there is a question about whether Mr. Klunck was armed at the time he was shot and, even if he was, whether it was necessary to shoot him.' So, guess what the police chief told the press? He issued a statement that the Internal Affairs investigator had concluded that the shooting was *justified!*

"Police can shape situations into anything they want. An honest cop called the Attorney General's office and told them the derringer was an alibi gun planted there by the police. That cop said APD had intended to mask the whole thing, but the coroner's office leaked information that Pete was shot in the back, so that put a crimp in their self-defense claim.

"The grand jury was told out-and-out lies, Lois! It took them seven minutes to come to the decision that there wasn't any evidence of wrong-doing. There was plenty of evidence, but it had been withheld from them! Can you imagine my fury and frustration? There I sat with all this material that pointed to murder and a police cover-up and nobody wanted to look at it!"

"So what did you do?" I asked her.

"I gave it to the newspapers and all the TV stations," she told me.

"So that's how the *Albuquerque Journal* got a copy of it!"

"Everybody wanted to kill me," Renee continued. "But by that time I didn't give a damn. The system can't be allowed to screw around with the truth like that! There's a huge drug operation going on in New Mexico, involving VIPs with control over law enforcement. That's what Peter found out about, and Kait may have too. I have a gut feeling there's a link between our children's cases."

Don and I returned from our trip to Albuquerque to find a letter from my agent saying that NBC had purchased film rights to one of my novels.

Ironically, the title was *Killing Mr. Griffin.*

CHAPTER EIGHT

In the spring of 1994, the paperback edition of *Who Killed My Daughter?* came out. That led to a fresh round of media blitz, and one of the shows I appeared on was *Sally Jessy Raphael.*

That show provided an 800 number for tipsters, and one of the calls was from a woman named Patricia Caristo.

The message she left for us was: "Do you know that a man with a record of violent crime, who was at your daughter's scene when police arrived, has never been interviewed?"

It turned out that Pat was a private investigator in Albuquerque, who, in 1992, had been retained by a law firm to conduct an accident reconstruction of Kait's shooting in respect to a possible motor-vehicle insurance claim. When Don and I declined to pursue that action, Pat's job was officially over, but by then she had become so intrigued by the case that she had not been able to let go of it.

"The crime scene appears to have been badly mishandled," she told Don and me during a three-way phone conversation. "When I read the reports, I was appalled. Not only was the man at the scene not interviewed, but there was evidence that wasn't followed up on, and no evidence hold was placed on Kait's car. When I saw you on television, still asking all the same questions I started asking two years ago, I felt that I had to get in touch with you."

"Who was the man at the scene?" Don asked her.

"His name is Paul Apodaca," Pat said. "He's a predator with a long record of violent attacks on women. In one case he abducted a woman, tied her up, and struck her repeatedly on the head with a baseball bat. Just three months before Kait's murder, Paul and a relative were arrested for negligent use of a handgun of the same small caliber that is thought to have killed Kait."

"What do you mean 'is *thought* to have killed Kait'?" I asked.

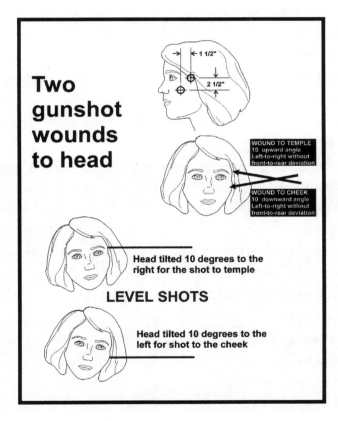

(Courtesy: Dean Garrison)

"Surely police could determine the caliber of the bullets."

"No bullets or casings were found," Pat said.

"But a bullet went into the door frame!"

"Only a tiny piece of it was found in the car—not enough to determine the caliber."

"The rest vanished into thin air?"

"Apparently so."

"Two bullets went into her head—"

"They weren't found either."

"But there weren't any exit wounds!" I exclaimed in bewilderment.

"The medical examiner told the Grand Jury—wait a minute, I've got his statement right here—" We could hear her shuffling papers. "He said, 'I recovered five very small bullet fragments along the wound tract. The larger portion of the bullet was not present in the body.'"

Bullet hole in the door frame of Kait's car.

It was too incredible to take in, so Don switched subjects.

"By 'the evidence that wasn't followed up on,' do you mean the beer can?"

"That's only part of it," Pat said. "Police say they were able to identify the location where Kait was shot by a large accumulation of broken glass. From there her car traveled over seven hundred feet, crossed the median and the opposite lane, went up onto the sidewalk and came to rest against a pole. It was found with the automatic transmission in park, and one of her shoes was on the ground outside the closed door on the driver's side."

"That's impossible," Don said. "Kait was in a coma. She couldn't have put the gear shift in park. And how would one of her shoes get outside the car?"

"That's a good question, since neither of the first two officers at the scene admits to opening the driver's door. Both say they went directly to the passenger's side, which is why they didn't notice the bullet hole in the doorframe. That bullet hole is another piece of evidence that wasn't taken seriously. Field investigators speculated that the hole was made by a larger caliber bullet than the ones that must have shattered in Kait's head. If true, that means two guns were used.

"I'm a former police officer and intelligence analyst. With your permission, I'd like to put together an analysis of the police investigation, based on the materials in the case file, and present it to the new police chief, Joseph Polisar. When I worked with the Intelligence Unit here in Albuquerque, Polisar was the supervisor, and he seemed to value the concept of analysis."

Pat did this work without charge and hand-delivered the seventy-five page report to the chief's office.

Pat Caristo. *(Courtesy: Gail Feldman)*

"Please, accept this analysis in the spirit in which it is offered," she said in her cover letter. "I have taken no actions that might compromise any on-going law enforcement investigation. I am at your disposal to discuss my analysis and the results of my investigation to date if you so desire."

Chief Polisar didn't respond.

In September, Don and I flew to Albuquerque to meet with Pat in person. By then we had checked out her background. The City of Philadelphia and the Philadelphia PD had commended her for heroism and both they and the UNM PD had awarded her commendations for meritorious performance before she moved on to become a private investigator.

This was enough to make us feel safe in her hands.

In person, this new recruit in Kait's Army turned out to be a vivacious brunette with a professional manner that was an interesting contrast to the laugh lines at the corners of her eyes and the array of family pictures on the shelf above her desk.[4]

"I have so many questions about the crime scene that I hardly know where to start," Pat told us. "We have an off-duty police officer—I'll call him Cop Number One—stumbling onto the scene minutes after the shooting. According to his report, when he first catches sight of the scene, he sees *two* cars, Kait's red car against the pole and *another car*. As he passes the scene, he radios headquarters to ask if an accident has been reported. The answer comes back negative, and he makes a U-turn and drives back to check things out. By that time the second car's gone, but Paul Apodaca is still there. Would you believe that nobody has ever raised the question of what that second car was doing there, who was in it, and why the driver took off when a cop showed up?

"Then Cop Number One radios in a report of an accident with no injuries."

"He does *what*?" I gasped.

"You heard me right. The second officer at the scene—we'll call

The garage where the VW Bug tried to take refuge.
(Photo by Lois Duncan)

her Cop Number Two—was dispatched to a 10-44, an accident with no injuries. And neither cop took information from Apodaca."

"Do you have any idea why?"

"I'm totally stymied. This case appears to have been compromised before the investigation started. You may be right when you speculated that Detective Gallegos was used as a scapegoat by his own department. At the start he was doing a fine job, interviewing all the right people and keeping good notes. Then it seems as if somebody closed him down. Crucial information in his field notes was withheld from his reports, and he destroyed all of his notes prior to discovery. Luckily for Miguel Garcia, his defense attorneys found copies of the notes in a file the police apparently forgot to purge. That's when the DA dropped the charges against the Hispanics."

"What sort of information was in those notes?" Don asked her.

"Things that indicate the shooting might not have been random. For example, Kait's next-door neighbor told Gallegos that Kait was followed from her apartment by a VW bug. That statement is in Gallegos's field notes, but not in his report."

"Michael Bush was puzzled by that too," I said. "Why would he withhold that important piece of information?"

"Perhaps his superiors wanted to close the case quickly?" Don suggested. "A thorough investigation would have taken a lot of manpower."

"The problem with that theory is that a cover-up seems to have started long before the complexities of the case became evident," Pat said. "Witnesses who lived a half block north of the scene reported being wakened by gun shots. They also reported seeing a VW bug with more than one person in it race up their street, pull into a lot next door to their house, turn off its lights, and after a short time make a U-turn and drive slowly back the same way it came. I started to wonder if the killers disposed of a weapon, so I decided to check to see if there was a Dumpster there. It turns out there was, but, more important, there's an auto body shop.[5] Police reports don't acknowledge the existence of that building. Why didn't they interview the owner of that business? They talked to the owners of other businesses in the area, so why omit *that* one? So many questions!"

"Michael talked with a P.I. who was investigating an auto repair shop," I said. "I wonder if this could be that shop."

I phoned the investigator, Roy Nolan, identified myself as a friend of Michael's, and asked him what, if anything, he knew about the body shop.

"I'm aware of that place," he responded cautiously. "Why are you interested?"

"We're hunting for a possible connection to our daughter's murder," I told him.

"Like I told Mr. Bush, you're looking at a crooked body shop where you take a wrecked car, they give you an exorbitant repair figure, and you give it to the insurance company," Nolan said. "From what I've observed, they also chop parts from stolen cars. In 1991, that shop was raided by the FBI, APD, ATF and the Department of Public Safety. They confiscated guns, and the owners' son was charged with drug dealing."

I handed the phone to Pat.

The two investigators talked for half an hour.

"Nolan's a gold mine of information," Pat told us after she hung up. "He had that shop under surveillance for weeks, and he says Vietnamese in expensive cars were always coming and going. In fact, he's established a link between the owner of that shop and a Vietnamese consultant for APD, whose son is a close friend of Dung's.

"The owner of the body shop also knew Kait. His girlfriend told Nolan they met Kait at a disco when Kait was there with a woman who fits the description of Susan Smith. Also, while Nolan was questioning the owner's girlfriend, he saw a newspaper article with a picture of Matt Griffin tacked up on the wall. The girlfriend told him the shop was a hangout for Griffin and other cops who held late night parties there. It's a lot to be coincidence—Vietnamese in fancy cars; a Vietnamese consultant for APD, whose son was one of Dung's buddies; the Ninja Bandit and his cop friends—all linked to a chop shop where drugs were sold and the owner knew Susan and Kait. And that's where the VW bug went after the shooting? It looks like we may have a tiger by the tail."

Since Pat was convinced that our answers lay at the crime scene, we decided that she should concentrate her main efforts there. We made up a list of people she should try to interview, including the first two officers at the scene, the medics who transported Kait to the hospital, and the witnesses who saw the VW bug pull into the parking lot. She would also try to locate Paul Apodaca, although that was not going to be easy, since the police had not obtained any identifiers.

We also decided it was time to take assertive action to get back the materials from Kait's desk.

The first thing Don and I did after leaving Pat's office was drive over to look at the body shop. It was a large multi-bay garage on a double lot. Along one side of the building and extending around behind it, there was a fenced area, the gate to which was padlocked.

Why had the VW bug gone straight to that site? Were the killers familiar with the area and aware of the Dumpster? Had they tossed a weapon into it? Had a passenger been dropped off? Had they planned to hide in the storage area and found it locked?

Back in 1990, when Juve Escobedo had abruptly vanished, I had asked Betty Muench to do a reading to see if he was dead. Betty had assured me that Juve was alive and said he was confined in a garage in Albuquerque.

"I don't get a sense that he's being held by the Vietnamese," she had said. "It seems like somebody in authority is acting independently without the people he works with knowing what he's doing."

That had made no sense at the time, but now, right here in front of us, was a garage that had been identified as a hangout for cops like Matt Griffin. On the day the bench warrant was issued for Juve's arrest, he had been on the phone with his girlfriend and suddenly told her, "Well, the police are outside now. The next time I talk to you,

I guess it will be from jail." Then he'd vanished and didn't reappear until the charges were dropped. Whatever those cops had come for, it wasn't to arrest him.

If they'd taken him somewhere, it certainly hadn't been to jail.

We'd given Pat power of attorney, and she was able to get permission to inventory Kait's personal belongings under the supervision of an evidence room technician. When she did so she found that the materials from Kait's desk were not there. According to the evidence room log, Detective Gallegos had misled us. Kait's personal belongings never had been entered into evidence.

Soon after that we received a call from a woman in Albuquerque with information about something else that was missing.

"I've come across one of your family videos," she told me.

The shock was so great that for a moment I couldn't get my breath.

"Where in the world did you find it?"

"At one of those places where you buy used tapes," the caller told me. "I don't usually look at those tapes before I record over them, but this time, for some reason, I decided to watch it, and there was *Donnie*! He and I went to school together, and I helped circulate your reward flyers. Kait appears on this tape, and before I erased it, I wanted to check and make sure you really didn't want it."

"We want it," I said. "Yes, we want it! God bless you for calling us!"

I told her where to mail it.

CHAPTER NINE

Another winter was upon us, bringing with it the holiday season and, like a blow to the heart, a new calendar. What right did it have to be 1995 when we had not yet closed the door on 1989? When we thought back upon the people that we had been immediately after Kait's death, reluctant to leave the house for fear of missing the call that would tell us her killers had been arrested, it was like remembering ridiculous overgrown children who still believed in Santa Claus. Back then there had been no way that we ever could have imagined that six years later we still would be waiting for that call.

The mystery of the missing videos continued to haunt us. They hadn't been lost after all, they were back in Albuquerque, and at least one of them had been discarded by whoever had taken them. But why would anyone want to steal those videos? The tape Donnie's friend had returned to us was mostly of a nephew's wedding. Toward the end of the tape Kait made a cameo appearance at a cookout, and we watched, spellbound, mesmerized by such simple wonders as the sight of her spilling catsup on her shirt and the sound of her voice squabbling with one of her brothers. But although such scenes evoked memories that were precious to us, there was nothing on tapes like that one to make it worth anyone's while to break into our house and take them.

But, then, we reminded ourselves, there had not been a break-in.

The thief had apparently had a key.

"Dung and his friends sometimes used Kait's car," Don said. "Our house key was on her key ring. It would have been easy for one of them to make a copy, and Dung knew where we kept the family videos. He used to watch them with Kait."

But what had been on those videos that made them worth stealing? We couldn't think of a thing.

In the spring, I was asked to serve as replacement for the dinner speaker at a convention of fraud investigators in Austin, Texas. Don suggested that I make a stopover in New Mexico to meet with the State Attorney General and make him aware of the problems we were having with the police investigation.

Pat set up the appointment and put together a packet of information. She also obtained tapes of all the interviews conducted by Miguel Garcia's defense attorneys and invited our new investigator friend, Roy Nolan, to meet with us to discuss them.

"It's no wonder Schwartz wasn't willing to prosecute," Pat told us. "The case against the Hispanics was non-existent. Even if the witnesses had been credible, which they weren't, the case would have been thrown out because of fabricated evidence. The police re-transcribed a tape to reverse its meaning. They couldn't have expected to get away with something that obvious. It's almost as if they wanted the Hispanic suspects to get off."

"Maybe they did," Nolan speculated. "All it took to shut down the investigation was an arrest. There didn't have to be a conviction."

"You think they may have arrested the Hispanics even though they knew they weren't guilty!" I exclaimed.

"That happens quite often," Nolan said. "A lot of times it's with the cooperation of the suspects. Most narcs have a stable of snitches who do whatever they're told to in exchange for protection from arrest for more serious crimes. People like that can earn money and favors by cooling their heels in jail for a while, knowing they'll never be convicted."

"But Miguel sat in jail for fifteen months!" I protested. "That's an awfully long time for a nineteen-year-old kid to 'cool his heels.'"

"He was due to serve that much time anyway for an unrelated burglary," Pat pointed out. "Schwartz dropped the burglary charges without explanation at the same time he dropped the homicide charges, so Miguel just traded one stint of jail time for another. And Juve didn't serve any time at all."

"Marty Martinez didn't serve time either," I said. "Police didn't even take a statement when he called and confessed. If the arrest of the Hispanics was just for show, and the police didn't want them to be prosecuted—"

"That would explain Marty's statement when he was questioned by the assistant DA," Pat said. "He said, 'The whole thing was a hoax, you know.'"

"Marty's confession would have wrecked the game plan," Nolan said. "Marty's a loose cannon. He may have been so drunk that night that he didn't remember afterward exactly what they'd been hired to do—intimidate Kait or kill her. All he knew was that he got paid a hundred dollars. The bottom line is, APD didn't want Marty confessing to murder for hire. They wanted him to shut up and go away."

"My question is, who controlled the investigation?" Pat said. "Who had the power to make the determination that the case was 'over' when the DA told police to investigate the Vietnamese?"

"What about the Vietnamese consultant whose son was Dung's friend?" I asked. "Would he have had that kind of influence?"[6]

LOIS DUNCAN

"That 'consultant' is in business with some very sleazy characters," Nolan told me. "One of them is under federal investigation
for trading gold for cocaine. Almost all major crime in this state
comes back to the drug scene. Small time dealers like Peter Klunck
get killed. The guys at the top are in high level political positions."

"None of that explains what went wrong at the scene," Pat said.
"*That's* where the cover-up started."

"I'll try to find out what happened that night," Nolan said.

"Be careful," Pat cautioned. "You don't want to rattle the wrong
cage."

"I know what I'm doing," Nolan told her. "I'll make a few calls
and get back with you. Where are you staying, Lois?"

I told him the name of my motel.

That night, reeling from jet lag, I went to bed early, only to be
jerked into consciousness several hours later by the blast of the telephone. I groped in the dark for the receiver, and when I finally located it, it took me a moment to recognize the staccato that ripped
into my ear as the voice of the unflappable, street smart investigator
with whom I had spent the afternoon.

"We were totally off base," Nolan said urgently. "The cops who
handled the crime scene are clean as the driven snow."

"How do you know?" I asked, still groggy with sleep.

"Just take my word for it," Nolan told me. "There wasn't a cover-
up, Lois. And we were wrong about the motive for Kait's murder. She
was the victim of a car-jacking."

"*What*?" I was fully awake now and couldn't believe what I was
hearing.

"Paul Apodaca was a car-jacker. That's the only thing that makes
sense."

102

"But what about the car wrecks and drug dealing?"

"The Vietnamese had nothing to do with this case," Nolan insisted. "And drugs didn't play any part in it. This was a car-jacking, pure and simple. There's no other possibility."

"I don't buy that," I said.

"You've got to believe me, Lois!"

"I don't buy it," I repeated and hung up the phone.

Nothing about the outrageous scenario was credible. Was I really supposed to believe that Paul Apodaca was standing on the sidewalk, drinking a Budweiser, and became so enamored of Kait's five year old Ford Tempo as she drove past that he shot her? Then he set his beer can down on the curb, leapt into his VW and drove to the auto body shop, where he disposed of his weapon in a Dumpster, made a U-turn and returned to the scene of the shooting, just in time to cozy up to an off duty police officer, while his own car left the scene all by itself without a driver?

Obviously something had happened since I'd last seen Nolan, and whatever it was had him terrified, either for himself or for me. In his effort to get information, he must have gone to the wrong person.

It struck me that I might have made a very bad mistake. I should have pretended to accept the car-jacking story. Now they—whoever the mysterious "they" might be—would have to find another way to convince me, and that might take a rougher form than a friendly phone call.

A chill swept over me as I envisioned one of Matt Griffin's buddies arriving at my door. How could I refuse to open up to the police? It was hard to imagine the type of person who could intimidate a man like Roy Nolan, and I wasn't in a hurry to find out.

I threw on my clothes, grabbed my suitcase, and left the motel room. The light above the doorway shone down like a spotlight, and I had never felt more vulnerable in my life than I did as I stood there fumbling in my purse for my car keys. I found them, got into the car, and pulled out of the parking lot onto a street as deserted as the one that Kait had been driving on the night she was shot. I could visualize the headline—*"Mother Imitates Daughter—Random Shootings Run In Family"*—a natural for the *National Enquirer*.

It seemed like forever before I spotted a motel with a vacancy sign. I pulled in and took a room for the remainder of the night, and the first thing in the morning, drove to the airport to trade in my eye-catching teal rental car for a car of a different make and color.

It was possible that Nolan had noticed what I was driving.

In my innocuous new vehicle—(I had specified that I wanted something "inconspicuous and grungy," a request that had not gone down well with the people at Avis)—I drove to Pat's office.

"Where have you been?" she demanded. "Roy Nolan has been trying to locate you. He says he's checked out all the cops connected with Kait's case, and they're clean as the driven snow. He tried to call you this morning, and when you didn't pick up he got worried. He asked me what kind of car you were driving."

"Why did he want to know that?"

"I don't know what he was thinking. Maybe he was going to try to look for you. He seemed very concerned that you'd left your motel without telling us."

"Did he tell you Kait was shot during a car-jacking?" I asked her.

"Of course not," Pat said. "That's ridiculous."

"We've lost Roy Nolan," I said.[7]

When I told her about Nolan's late night phone call, she shook her head in bewilderment.

"Maybe he'd been drinking?" she suggested.

"He didn't sound drunk, he sounded frantic."

That was the day we were scheduled to meet with the State Attorney General, but that didn't happen. He stood us up, and we were relegated to a new assistant AG who reluctantly accepted Pat's case materials. We knew when we left his office that we wouldn't be hearing from him.

Faced with an unexpected block of free time, I decided to pay a visit to Renee Klunck. The federal grand jury had now concluded their civil rights investigation of Peter's death and no indictments had been returned. According to a statement by the U.S. Attorney, the case was too old and there was too much conflicting testimony to charge Griffin or any member of the police department with criminal conduct. "Accurate recollections fade with time," he said. "No one can now say with certainty exactly what happened on the morning of January 27, 1989."

Renee, though disappointed, had accepted the inevitable.

"At least, they didn't find the shooting justified," she said.

"Did Peter ever mention an auto repair shop on Arno Street?" I asked her as we settled ourselves at her breakfast bar with our cups of coffee.

"Not that I recall," Renee said, but the Kluncks' youngest son Danny, who had wandered into the kitchen to make himself a sandwich, overheard the question.

"I know where that is," he said. "Pete used to do off-the-books body work for those people. I know he worked at that shop in December of 1988, because that's where he took the dents out of my car."

"But that would mean—" Renee sent her coffee cup crashing to the counter as the significance of that statement hit her. "That would mean that, one month before Griffin shot him, Peter was working at a location where Griffin hung out! For six years the cops have insisted there was no possible way that Griffin and Peter could have known each other. Now we find out they were right in each other's pockets!"

"Do you know if Peter had Vietnamese friends?" I asked Danny.

"No, but Griffin did," he told me. "The first time I ran into Griffin, before all this shit came down, he was in a parking lot in the Northeast Heights with a bunch of guys on motorcycles. A lot of those bikers were Vietnamese."

At the end of the day I flew to Austin to speak at the conference of fraud specialists. Michael Bush flew in from L.A. to provide emotional support, bringing with him his friend Leslie Kim, the editor of a national trade paper for insurance claims investigators.

The investigators were an intimidating group to speak to, especially when I discovered that the speaker I was there to replace was Texas Governor George W. Bush. After my presentation I asked for questions and was confronted by stony silence from a roomful of deadpan, primarily male, investigators. Too drained and discouraged to make even a token attempt at socializing, I made my apologies to Michael and his editor friend and headed up to my hotel room.

"By the way," Michael told me as we said our "good nights" at the elevator, "I had the weirdest call this morning from Roy Nolan. I think that guy must have blown a batch of brain cells. He kept trying to convince me that Kait was the victim of a car-jacking."

CHAPTER TEN

John Cooke Fraud Report, April 1995:

A CHILD IS DEAD, A FAMILY STILL MOURNS
WHO KILLED KAITLYN ARQUETTE?

On March 4, 1995, almost six years after losing her youngest child to what the Albuquerque Police Department terms (to this very day) a random, drive-by shooting, Lois Arquette spoke before the Texas International Association of Special Investigation Units at their annual seminar.

Speaking in front of nearly 300 investigators, it was clear that her need for an answer to this tragedy was paramount to an eventual healing of the wounds. . . .

Nearly an hour later, she stopped and asked if the audience had any questions.

Silence. Deafening silence.

She looked around the room and saw no hands raised. Later, she confided to me that she thought that the lack of response was due to disinterest. She could not have been more mistaken. What Arquette thought was disinterest was instead attributable to the overwhelming effect she had on that crowd of big, tough investigators.

The front-page article, illustrated by a photo of Kait's grave, contained a footnote by the editor:

While we still do not know who killed Kaitlyn Arquette, we do know that her death was far more than a random drive-by shooting. The answer may be buried beneath the tens of thousands of suspicious auto accidents that are crammed into our collective insurance industry files.

At the conclusion of Arquette's speech, one of the people in the audience made an incredibly generous offer. This family-owned company that owns a proprietary database of over 160 million name-search entries has donated as much on-line time as we need to assist in the solving of this crime. Two weeks ago, claims investigator Jim Ellis, sat in our office and began the massive task of running the information. . . .

Leslie Kim shipped me a hundred copies of the article, and I sent them to everyone I could think of including the FBI, the U.S. Attorney, the Attorney General, the INS, and the claims department of every insurance company in Albuquerque.

Only one person responded—Charlie Parsons, Special Agent in Charge of the L.A. Office of the FBI. The FBI had recently assumed federal jurisdiction in both automobile accident fraud schemes and Medicare fraud, as well as Vietnamese organized crime in the United States. Agent Parsons wrote me that, based upon the information provided by us and our investigators, their office was opening an official investigation of the subjects in California who were participants in the fraud ring.

I mailed a copy of Agent Parsons' letter to the FBI office in Albuquerque.

"I accept that you can't become officially involved in the

investigation of Kait's murder unless APD invites you in," I said. "One would hope, however, that the fact that the FBI in L.A. has initiated an investigation of this crime ring may bring you into this situation by the back door."

They did not respond.

Once again we were at a plateau as far as the case went, but we didn't feel alone in our impotence. The flood of mail from readers of my book had accelerated since the publication of the paperback, and I spent many hours each day responding to letters:

"Our daughter, Natalie, was killed by a shotgun blast to the head in the presence of her jealous boyfriend, an officer with the local police department. His own department performed the investigation and labeled the death a suicide. Natalie, who was breaking up with the boyfriend, had been out that night with another man, and the boyfriend had been tailing her. After the shooting, the boyfriend pried Natalie's teeth out of the bedroom wall and carried them in his mouth during the funeral. To us, this does not seem like normal behavior. We do not believe Natalie killed herself."

"Two years ago my best friend and both her daughters were murdered. She was suffocated. Her twelve-year-old was strangled with a phone cord and raped, and the three-year-old was drowned in the bathtub in an inch of water. Evidence was destroyed because a sheriff deputy's son was accused, (his prints were found on the bathtub). My friend comes to me in dreams, crying and wanting to know why."

There also were letters that renewed my faith in humanity:

"I am a 17-year-old girl who lives in San Diego. I am one of the Vietnamese boat people and proud of my heritage, except I am shameful of the conduct of some of my fellow refugees. I am afraid for my life when I am in Little Saigon after dark. My mother's hairdresser was gunned down by the Vietnamese Mafia. Storekeepers close shop early for fear of being robbed and killed. The fear this community has is fear of retaliation. It's a catch 22—tell and hope that justice will prevail— don't tell and keep your family alive.

"Thank you for writing your book. You have taken one of the first steps in unveiling organized Vietnamese crime to the general public and in turning the legal wheels that will one day make Little Saigon and all other Vietnamese communities safe again."

Then, three days short of Kait's twenty-fifth birthday, I received a very different sort of letter with the return address of a federal correction facility:

"Compassionate Lois, peace be upon you,

My name is Lawrence*, I am presently incarcerated at the above stated institution. Back in 1987 through June 1989, me and your daughter Kait used to correspond. I found her name and address in a correspondence magazine. She claimed she was 19, when in reality, as I later found out, she was only 16. She said if I answered her letter I should address it in care of a girlfriend because her parents wouldn't approve. I did respond, and we continued to correspond."

This scenario struck me as plausible. Over the years, Kait had

had many pen pals. When she was sixteen a sudden surge of mail had alerted us to the fact that she had listed her address in a singles magazine and lied about her age. We insisted that she remove the ad, and the letters stopped coming. As far as we knew that was the end of it. But, as headstrong as Kait had been, it was perfectly in character for her to have continued a clandestine correspondence.

I continued reading:

"Kait told me about the activities her boyfriend Dung was involved in. She told me she was frightened, she felt used and trapped, and Dung's friends had warned her to keep quiet or they'd harm her entire family. In the last letter I got from her in mid-June, 1989, she told me she had reached the end of her rope and was going to report Dung and his friends to the authorities. I never heard from her again. Her girlfriend wrote and told me Kait had been killed. There is much we need to discuss. I believe I can tell you who the trigger man is."

Then there came the inevitable request for money:

"Before I get into the details of what I know about your daughter's murder, let me explain that I am a complete pauper. I am in dire need of stamps, cigarettes, gym shoes, etc. I also need to purchase important legal books. If you would immediately send me funds to help me obtain these necessities I would truly appreciate it. Any amount, be it a dime or a thousand dollars, would be appreciated."

Lawrence then baited the hook with the statement that Kait's girlfriend knew about all the things Kait had been planning to expose and had shared her information with him before fleeing

Albuquerque because her life had been threatened.

"*She told me there were two triggermen and she named them,*" he said. "*She told me she originally planned to be with Kait that night, and she was lucky she wasn't.*"

I sent him a money order for one hundred dollars.

Back came his thank you note:

"*Thank you for the $100. I am truly grateful. But in no way will that cover the cost of my present needs. I must ask that you send me a money order for $900. If you honor this request I'll send you information that can and will get the killers and those who assisted them convicted.*"

He, then, extended a carrot that was irresistible:

"*Kait's girlfriend told me Kait had a fake friend, a white female, who set her up to be shot by being sure that within a certain time frame she'd drive down Lomas. Two Spanish guys with the same last name were paid to stalk and kill her.*"

How long should I keep on going with this? The man was a cold-blooded opportunist, but that didn't mean that his information wasn't valid. We knew that Susan Smith had fled the state in fear for her life, and Paul Apodaca had the same last name as his brother Mark, who had recently been convicted of an unrelated murder.

I sent him another hundred.

"*I request your permission to tell you something confidential*

about Kait," Lawrence now wrote me. "Your daughter was undergoing
very serious problems she feared to confess to anybody except me. She
was coerced to get indirectly involved with something she didn't desire
to do. I was horrified when I heard about it.

"I appreciate the second $100 money order. You now owe me only
$800. This is very reasonable considering all that I know about Kait's
awful secret which could solve this case for you."

I wondered if Kait's "awful secret" involved the importation of
drugs. After all, she had worked as supervisor of imported clothing
at a store where most of the merchandise came from the Orient.

I decided to get Pat's advice before proceeding any further. I
reached for the phone and discovered that my left hand wouldn't
close around the receiver.

"Oh, no, not again!" I tried to say, and the words came out as
gibberish.

It was forty miles on a two-lane road to the nearest hospital, and
Don got me there in just over half an hour. During that long wild
ride I regained my speech, but I kept losing parts of my anatomy.
First my left arm fell limp. Then my left leg. I was braced for my right
side to start kicking in. Was anything going to be left by the time we
reached the hospital?

But once again I was lucky. By the following morning my leg
was working. It was several months before I could raise my left arm
above shoulder level and over a year before I could type with my left
hand, but I eventually got most of myself back.

Brain scans revealed no indication of a stroke, and the doctors
concluded the paralysis had been caused by a massive, stress in-
duced seizure that had trashed my nervous system. They said I must

learn to relax, and I promised to try, but Lawrence wasn't making that easy. His letters continued to pour in, with intimate revelations about Kait's personal idiosyncrasies, some of which were disconcertingly accurate; and with ferocious demands for money.

Plus the constant titillating offers of important information:

"My sources in Albuquerque have now located Kait's girlfriend. She has sent me the diary that Kait kept from 1987 through 1989. You know Kait's handwriting, so when I send it to you, you'll know it's hers. Where is my $800?"

Pat ran a Federal Correction Department search on Lawrence's name and prison I.D. number. It came up negative. She contacted the federal correctional facility to which I had been addressing my letters. This too came up negative.

Officially, Lawrence didn't exist.

"But he has to be there!" I protested. "That's where I write to him!"

"He might be in a witness protection program," Pat speculated. "One of the methods the government uses to protect such people is to channel their mail through prison drop boxes."

That was not an appealing idea, as it meant Lawrence might not be incarcerated at all and be out there right now, camping in a pup tent behind one of our bayberry bushes, watching us through the windows.

"Where's my money?" he continued to write in an increasingly hysterical frenzy. *"What kind of mother are you that you don't want Kait's diary and you're not even interested in her secret!"*

At the end of her patience, Pat forwarded that letter to the prison. The warden allowed that Lawrence was, indeed, an inmate there, whose crimes ranged from kidnapping to rape to aggravated assault. He described my pen pal as "a very large, violent, clever, jail-house lawyer," a problem prisoner who was often in the "hole" because of his continued violent acts within the prison.

"That's to our advantage," Pat said. "Lawrence is currently in solitary, which means the warden will be able to get at his stuff. Prisoners have their rights to privacy, and their possessions are off limits unless they're in solitary. Since Lawrence is in the hole, his property is in prison control and can be searched. The warden has agreed to see if he's got Kait's diary."

Prison officials confiscated Lawrence's belongings. Although they found no diary, they did find clippings of articles from Albuquerque papers that must have been sent to him by an accomplice in New Mexico. There was also a file of clippings about other unsolved murders and drafts of letters extorting money from the victims' families.

"Compassionate Doris, peace be with you," one of them said. *"Back in 1993 and 1994, me and your daughter Kippy used to correspond, and she told me a terrible secret. . . ."*

Reading that letter and visualizing Kippy's poor mother, I was violently sick to my stomach.

Soon after that, I experienced that same reaction when Paul Apodaca suddenly hit the headlines:

Albuquerque Journal, October 5, 1995

MAN RAPES STEPSISTER TO GET INTO PRISON

An Albuquerque man told the judge he raped his 14-year-old stepsister so he could go to prison to protect a younger brother imprisoned on a murder conviction. Judge Richard Knowles obliged with a 20-year sentence for Paul Raymond Apodaca, but recommended to the Department of Corrections that Apodaca not be housed in the same prison as his brother."

By now Pat had interviewed the first two officers at Kait's scene. Their statements conflicted so radically that they might have been at two different crime scenes. Each blamed the other for not taking information from Apodaca. Cop Number One said he assigned that job to Cop Number Two, because, "I had to make a choice—I had to stay with the injured person." Cop Number Two was adamant that Cop Number One had specifically told her *not* to take information from Apodaca, because he already had done so. Cop Number Two told Pat that, as soon as she suspected murder, she called her supervisor. Yet the supervisor recalled no call from Cop Number Two and said the person who called her was Cop Number One.

Pat went down to the detention center to get Apodaca's version of the story.

"The first thing he asked was, 'How did you find me?'" she told us. "He apparently thought the police reports had made him untraceable."

When she questioned him about his presence at the scene, he

Paul Raymond Apodaca—Registered Sex-Offender.

explained he was in the neighborhood to buy drugs from a friend named Lee. He described how he and Cop Number One had gone together to look into Kait's car, but denied ever seeing Cop Number Two, although Cop Number Two had told Pat that she was with the two men when they went to Kait's car and had described Apodaca's excitement at the sight of so much blood.

Apodaca went on to say he had given Cop Number One his name and then driven off in his car—a VW bug—and gone around the corner to his drug dealer's house. According to Apodaca, he remained with Lee for about half an hour, and when he left he noticed an ambulance at the scene.

Pat recognized Lee's name from a public records report of Apodaca's 1990 arrest for shooting a prostitute from his VW bug. At the time of that incident, Apodaca had presented Lee's MVD identification card, apparently assuming that Lee would be immune to arrest.

Pat went to Lee's home, and his mother answered the door and said Lee was sleeping. When Pat identified herself as a private investigator who was working on the Arquette case, the woman responded, "You mean the girl who was shot by those Vietnamese guys?" Lee's mother confirmed that Paul Apodaca was a close friend of Lee's and promised to give Lee Pat's card.

She also proudly volunteered the fact that her other son was an APD narcotics officer.

CHAPTER ELEVEN

Highlights of 1996:

Jim Ellis retired.

Michael Bush and his wife became parents of a little boy.

Pat Caristo became the grandmother of a little girl.

Don began doing volunteer work for Habitat for Humanity.

Kerry wrote her first book and won the Colorado Young Readers Award.

Both Robin and Brett got married.

Donnie won $11,000 playing a slot machine on an Indian reservation.

As for me—I dreamed.

What I dreamed about was Kait's diary.

During daylight hours I obsessed about that diary. With Lawrence now out of the picture, I would never know if Kait's journal actually existed. Despite the fact that the man was a sadistic con artist, his information about Kait's personal life had been disturbingly accurate. He had known that, at age sixteen, she had posted an ad in a singles magazine and misrepresented her age by three years. That was not a specific you pulled out of a hat. If Lawrence himself was a fraud, then he had to have obtained information from somebody who knew Kait.

Either that, or his conspirator had access to her diary.

One night before falling asleep, I said to Kait, "I'm going to sleep with my mind propped open. I want you to try to get into it and tell me what's in that diary. If there isn't any diary, then tell me what you would have written in a diary if you'd kept one."

That night I had a vivid dream in which Kait appeared, shaken and teary-eyed, and announced that she had been raped. Then, suddenly I was reading an account of that rape in a journal. The entry was worded in third person, as if the author was trying to distance herself from the violence, and it ended with the sentence, "Then Katie sat down and read a magazine." At the bottom of the page there was a little stick-on heart like the ones our grandchildren liked to paste on envelopes. In the dream I reached out and touched the heart, and it came off in my hand. I turned it over, and on the back there was the name "Roxanne."

I woke up with a start and lay, staring into the darkness, trying to discern the meaning of this extraordinary message—if, indeed, it was a message. We had no reason to believe that Kait had been sexually assaulted, and I wasn't aware of any friend of hers named Roxanne. Kait had been an avid reader when it came to novels, but the only place she read magazines was under the hair dryer.

Kait's purse had been returned to us by the hospital and contained a date book with a page in the back for phone numbers. I kept that book in the bottom drawer of my dresser. Now, I got out of bed and groped in the drawer for the book, which I carried into the bathroom so I could turn on the light and read without waking

Don. The calendar revealed that, on the week of her death, Kait had had not one, but two, appointments with her hairdresser, one for a haircut and the other for *"pictures with Roxanne."*

I flipped to the back of the book and found the number for the beauty parlor. In the morning I dialed it and asked to speak to "Roxanne." The receptionist told me that nobody named Roxanne was employed there. Then a voice in the background called out, "There was a Roxanne who used to work here. I think she quit to start her own shop." I asked what Roxanne's last name was, but nobody could remember.

I phoned Pat and told her about the heart dream.

"I think Kait wants us to talk to her hairdresser," I said.

Pat was kind enough not to scoff, but she wasn't exactly jumping up and down with excitement.

"You don't know where Roxanne works or what her last name is?"

"No," I said. "But I do think we need to find her."

"I'll see what I can do," Pat said without much enthusiasm.

Several days later, she called me, sounding stunned.

"I found Roxanne," she said. "You're not going to believe this! Roxanne has a *heart tattoo* on her upper arm!"

Roxanne told Pat that she had been more than Kait's hairdresser, the two had been personal friends. Kait had babysat for Roxanne's children, and Roxanne had used Kait for a hair model, which accounted for the notation *"pictures with Roxanne."* And, not only had Roxanne cut Kait's hair, she also had cut Dung's hair.

"I asked her if she had a problem understanding Dung's English, since that's the reason the police gave for not being able to properly question him," Pat said. "Roxanne said she understood him fine, except on the night Kait was shot. She said he phoned her a little before midnight, babbling, 'Kait's dead! They shot Kait!' He was so hysterical that she had to keep asking him to repeat himself."

"He called her *before midnight?*" I exclaimed. "But he wasn't told about the shooting until three the next morning! Is she certain about the time?"

"Her husband's confirmed it. They'd just watched the evening news and were getting ready for bed. If that's true, it means Dung knew about the shooting three hours before police informed him. And it sounds like he knows who did it. He didn't say, 'Kait's been shot,' he said, 'They shot Kait!'"

"Roxanne also knew about the car wreck scam," Pat continued. "She said Kait was very upset about Dung's activities and wanted out of the relationship. Kait also told her that Dung's group was stealing cars and changing the engine numbers, which would certainly be a reason for them to frequent that body shop. Roxanne said she tried to give that information to Detective Gallegos, but he told her she wasn't telling him anything he didn't already know."

"Is Roxanne willing to sign an affidavit?"

"She's eager to do that. She's always wondered why the police wouldn't take a statement from her. Oh, and one other thing—I just had a call from a woman named Linda, whose son, Nathan Romero, was murdered in Albuquerque in 1993. Linda thinks his case may link to Kait's."

She gave me Linda's number, and I immediately dialed it.

"Nathan was chased down by three cars, stabbed, and left to die in the street," Linda told me. "He was found with a Vietnamese medallion clutched in his hand, apparently snatched from his killer during the struggle. APD didn't bother to place that medallion into evidence. It was turned over to me along with Nathan's personal effects."

Friends who had been with Nathan had identified his killers, but the police had refused to arrest them.

"That Asian gang harassed me for years," Linda said. "The men were so cocky they'd park in front of my house and sit there grinning. They'd laugh at Nathan's friends and ask them if they wanted to be killed next. Even when two gang members came forward as witnesses, APD didn't make arrests. During one phone conversation, a police captain got so furious with me that he bellowed at the top of his lungs, 'We know who killed your son just like we know who killed Kait Arquette! This is police business—butt out!' When I asked him why he was connecting those two cases, he yelled at me to keep my mouth shut and forget I ever heard that."

Linda refused to be intimidated and informed her private investigator, who contacted the mayor and warned him that the City could expect a massive law suit if the police didn't do their job.

"Then things started to happen," Linda told me. "The case detective, Steve Gallegos—wasn't he your case detective too?—got transferred out of the department, and Nathan's killers were arrested. Not that it did much good, because they plea bargained."

When I asked Linda the name of the APD captain who had linked our children's cases, it turned out to be the same captain who had stated on "Good Morning, America" in regard to Kait's case, "The Vietnamese angle was extensively looked into. We could find no tie to the homicide with any Vietnamese gang."

Meanwhile, our family was experiencing happy times also, for in the course of two months we had acquired a daughter-in-law and

Kerry rejoicing with Robin at her wedding.
(Courtesy: William Steinmetz)

a second son-in-law. Brett and his girlfriend Cindy eloped to Las Vegas, while Robin was married to Anatole in a small but joyous ceremony in a garden in Florida. We were worried about the weather because it had been raining off and on all day, but when the bride stepped under the arbor, radiant with happiness and more beautiful than we ever had seen her, the sun broke through the clouds and the sky was split by a rainbow. Kerry, who was matron-of-honor, stood slightly apart from her sister to acknowledge the space where Kait would have stood if she had been there. When I looked at that space I was almost able to convince myself that—for just an instant—it was occupied by the misty form of a girl in a peach color dress the same shade as Kerry's. Then the image was gone, and I accepted it as a trick of the light and an overactive imagination.

That evening, after the newlyweds left on their honeymoon, the rest of us reminisced about happy times and sad ones. Kait was very much on our minds.

"Since the cops don't want your information, why don't we put it on the Internet?" Brett suggested. "Maybe somebody out there will read and react to it."

Brett, who was a computer guru, designed the website, which included a message board and e-mail envelope for informants.[8]

He posted the page, and surfers found it. Steve Schiff, United States Congressman from New Mexico, called to suggest that we request an Internal Affairs investigation. I told him we had little confidence in the APD Internal Affairs Unit, since a former supervisor—an alleged field officer at Kait's scene—had been charged with burglarizing a liquor store.

"Good point," Schiff acknowledged. "Let's try to go over their heads then." He wrote a letter to Attorney General Janet Reno, requesting that the Justice Department look into a possible police cover-up. The Civil Rights Division responded that the federal five-year statute of limitations prohibited their doing that.

"I'm sorry I couldn't do more for you," Congressman Schiff told us. "I do have one suggestion. Under New Mexico law, the State Attorney General can prosecute a case where the local district attorney declines. As the DA has not charged the individual you suspect, I recommend you contact the AG's office."

It was a well-meant suggestion from a good and caring man, who didn't realize that the Attorney General wouldn't meet with us. And even if Congressman Schiff could convince him to do so, whom would we accuse of Kait's murder? Dung Nguyen? An Quoc Le? Bao Tran? Paul Apodaca? A hired hit man who might or might not have been Miguel Garcia? As private citizens, neither we nor Pat had the authority to force witnesses and suspects to talk to us. Only the police could do that.

The traffic at Kait's website continued to accelerate, and many of those visitors contacted us by e-mail. Among them were a forensic expert from Illinois and a crime scene technician from Michigan, both of whom offered to review Kait's scene information. They asked us to send them copies of the scene reports, autopsy report, and a full set of crime scene photos.

We were able to provide them with everything except the pictures and set out to get those by submitting an Inspection of Public Records Act request. The APD photo lab told us that nine rolls of pictures had been taken but only a couple of shots on each roll had turned out. We ordered two sets of the twenty-two photos. The charge for those snapshot size prints was $176.

I was not prepared for the impact those photos would have on me. Although Kait was not in the pictures, her blood was sloshed on the seat and floorboards of the car. There was a large pool of body liquids on the curb next to the passenger's door, and a small black object that looked like a shoe lay on the ground outside the closed door on the driver's side.

I opened the packet while standing at the mailbox and trudged up the driveway to the house, clutching the photos to my chest. Since Don was not home, and I had to reach out to somebody, I e-mailed the technician in Michigan.

He responded instantly: "Lois, Lois, Lois, it's a grim business, this. It's not for anyone who ever loved the victim. We hope the pictures tell a story, but it's probably not a story you should have to read or can read. It's told in the language of blood and broken glass and bullet holes. Put those pictures away for now. I'll let you know my reaction when I receive my set."

I went into the bedroom and buried my face in a pillow and screamed until the back of my throat felt like I'd swallowed lye. Because I *could* read the language of broken glass and bullet holes, not with the mind of a criminalistics expert, but with the heart of a mother. I could see my daughter in that car, gripping the steering wheel, frozen with horror as a bullet crashed into the door frame next to her head, and there was no place to run, no place to hide, and Mother and Daddy just a few miles away in that big safe house, and no way to reach them. If only I had been with her! In my mind I rewrote the story so I was seated beside her and could grab that shiny gold head and yank it down below window level. In that vision I threw myself across her and leaned on the horn. People came rushing to windows, came pouring out of buildings, came racing to save this terrified girl, who by now I had somehow managed to shove down to the floor boards. When the other shots came—(*if* they came, for perhaps the killers would be frightened off by the commotion)—I would be the one to receive them. And, oh, I would receive them gladly! I would smile as I slid into darkness knowing that Kait would survive to go to college, to become a doctor, to meet and marry Prince Charming, to have children just as ornery and strong-willed and naughty and wonderful as she was, and to live and live and live.

"I want her back!" I shrieked into the muffling mound of the pillow. "I want her back!"

Then finally I cried.

Eventually I must have fallen asleep from exhaustion, because the next thing I knew I was sprawled on the bed in a room that was gentled by twilight, and the sound of the TV in the living room told

Kait's shoe on ground outside driver's side door.

me that Don had returned and was watching the 6:00 p.m. news.

I sat up and turned on the light and spread out the photos on the bed. The object on the ground was, indeed, Kait's shoe. Since the first two officers at the scene had stated that they had gone to the passenger's side, I wondered if the killer might have opened the driver's door to check and make sure she was done for. If so, it was possible that either he—or Paul Apodaca, if Paul wasn't the killer himself—had cleaned out her purse. That purse had been returned to us at the hospital, and when I opened Kait's wallet I'd been surprised that it contained no money. I knew that Kait had had cash when she'd left our house that night, because she had mentioned her plan to buy ice cream to take to Susan's. Susan had said Kait didn't arrive with ice cream.

We mailed the reconstructionists copies of the photos, and both were puzzled by their limited number and poor quality.

"Are you saying that they were not able to take more than

twenty-two pictures out of all those exposures?" asked the cop in Illinois. "Where are the shots of the large concentration of glass that was used to determine the spot where the shots were fired? If auto glass found at the scene was considered important enough to measure and describe, there should be photographs of it along with evidence markers."

Our consultants were also frustrated by the fact that there were no well-lighted, close-up, scale photos of Kait's car.

"There ought to be photos that include a scale or ruler and are labeled with markers," they told us. "Once the scene work was completed, the car would have been removed to a secure location for a detailed search, latent print processing, and photography. There should be at least one roll of film showing that process."

We contacted APD and were told there were no daylight photos, no pictures with scale markers, and no pictures of the pile of glass. No photos existed other than the ones we'd been given.

Then, something happened to convince us that wasn't the truth.

The crime scene analysts had asked to see televised news footage, so one evening, while I was fixing dinner, Don set out to make copies of our videos of TV coverage.

Suddenly he shouted, "Come see what I've found on *Sightings!*"

I rushed in from the kitchen, and he backed up the tape and reran it. An image flashed onto the screen and immediately vanished. It was there for only an instant, but that was long enough.

"That's Kait's car!" I exclaimed. "And the photo was taken in *daylight!*"

"Hang on," Don told me. "There's a better image coming up."

There it was—another daylight APD photo of Kait's car that zeroed in on a close-up of the bullet hole in the doorframe. That hole had a piece of evidence tape positioned above it, which did not appear in the photos that we had been given.

We sent the video to the crime scene technician in Michigan, who scanned the frames and transferred them to discs. Neither of our consultants was able to tell much from the grainy images.

"What these do reveal, however, is that APD has been holding out on you," one told us. "Keep asking for copies of the photos. I'm sure there are people in APD who refer to you as 'that nutty Arquette woman,' but somewhere you may run into someone who sees this as a noble search for the truth."

Don submitted a second request, asking for all the case photos that had not been provided to us. The supervisor of the photo lab responded that there now appeared to be only four rolls of negatives in Kait's file, as compared to the nine rolls that had been there previously.

"I don't understand what's going on," she commented. "We don't have the things we ought to have."

She had those eighty photos printed for us. All turned out to be night scenes and none showed the broken glass or evidence markers. Don reiterated that our request was for *all* photos taken by APD of the crime scene and of Kait's car, including the daylight images with the evidence tape.

The lab relayed that request to the legal department and was told to inform us case photos were not public record. Then, one hundred and twenty-six more photos mysteriously surfaced. None had been taken in daylight and none showed the glass.

The new batch of photos contained shots of Kait in the hospital. As I gazed at the bloated face that had once been so beautiful and at the poor shaven head encased in bloody bandages, I recalled Bob

Schwartz's statement about his view of reality.

"A prosecutor's reality is not defined by truth," he had told me. "It's a refined and screened and artificial version of it."

There was nothing refined about the content of these photographs. I ran my finger across Kait's shattered temple and traced the curve of the ravished cheek, as if by touch I could magically make them whole again.

These were *my* reality.

The fact that police had taken daylight pictures of Kait's car, revealing evidence tape that wasn't in any of the scene photos, indicated a second day work-up that wasn't on record.

The Criminalistics Supervisor in charge of Kait's scene was no longer with APD and now lived out of state. He told Pat on the phone that he had not seen any pile of glass and thought the "trail of glass" referred to in scene reports might just have been fragments and could not even have been determined to have come from a particular vehicle. He had no explanation for the "No Evidence Hold" note in the case file and acknowledged that there *had* been a second day work-up. He said reports of that work-up had been sent to the case detectives and to the records department. He didn't recall that his team had found anything significant or taken any photographs.

But the picture with the evidence marker indicated that they *had* taken photos, whether the supervisor remembered that or not. And a homicide detective had confided to Robin's girlfriend Maritza that the location of a bullet found "later, not during the initial investigation," had proved that the shooting was a "hit."

Was it possible that Criminalistics had found more than a fragment of the bullet that penetrated the doorframe, and that bullet was

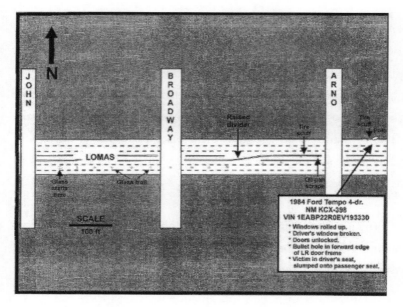

Map of crime scene. *(Courtesy: Dean Garrison)*

of a larger caliber than the bullets that fragmented in Kait's head? Since the investigative units appeared to be compartmentalized, it was probable that Criminalistics would not have been aware of the findings of the medical examiner. But the detectives in the homicide department, who were coordinating information and picking and choosing which reports to place in Kait's case file, would have been acutely aware of what they were looking at if evidence indicated those bullets were different sizes. Two individuals, firing different caliber weapons, could not be considered "random shooters."

And what about the "large accumulation of broken glass" that suddenly now had become undistinguishable fragments that might not even have come from Kait's car?

"Maybe there *was* no glass in the street," Don speculated. "Perhaps Kait was *not* shot at that junction."[9]

Our only hope of obtaining the rest of the photographs seemed to be to file a suit against the police department. So we made another trip to Albuquerque to meet with attorneys to see what our legal options were. We were up front about the fact that our goal was to take the case to court so we could subpoena copies of the case materials.

One attorney after another told us they weren't interested.

The last one we met with was compassionate enough to tell us why.

"No attorney will take on this case with that stipulation," he said. "True, there are those of us who have built our practices on suing the police, but we always settle out of court with no admission of wrongdoing. That's the way it's done here."

Once again, we submitted a request for the return of the materials from Kait's desk. This time we channeled that request through the APD Legal Department, who sent a legal assistant to the evidence room. She found, as Pat had done, that Kait's things weren't there. However, she continued to investigate and eventually discovered a closet safe in the Violent Crimes Unit which contained all the "lost" materials from Kait's desk.

Pat insisted on being there when the safe was opened and attempted to reclaim Kait's personal belongings for us. She was thwarted by Detective Gallegos, who belatedly had everything placed into evidence.

CHAPTER TWELVE

So many questions screamed for answers, but there was one that could never be answered by posting it on the Internet. It was the source of my dream about a heart named "Roxanne."

Where had that image come from?

Much as I wanted to accept the dream as proof that consciousness continues after death and that those who pass over retain the ability to communicate with loved ones, my skeptical nature was my enemy. A nagging voice in the back of my mind kept telling me it was far more likely that at some point Kait had mentioned to me that her hairdresser had a heart tattoo. The fact that I didn't recall such a conversation didn't mean that it hadn't taken place and the memory had been stored in my subconscious. Having that memory surface in a dream and lead us to valuable information could have been mere coincidence.

I phoned Roxanne to thank her for telling Pat about Dung's phone call.

"I hope that it helps," Roxanne said. "Kait didn't deserve what happened to her. She told me about the staged car wreck. Dung didn't tell her about it until after he'd done it."

"You mean Kait wasn't in on it?" I felt as if a weight had been lifted from my heart.

"Definitely not," Roxanne assured me. "They had a big fight

134

about it. She agreed to give Dung one more chance to shape up and get a real job and break with those awful friends of his. Like I told Detective Gallegos, I don't believe Dung killed Kait, but I'm certain he knows who did."

"Did Pat Caristo tell you about my dream?" I asked her.

"That's so bizarre!" Roxanne exclaimed. "And what's even weirder is that I'd only just gotten that tattoo. I'd had it about a week when Pat came to see me."

That revelation was so startling that it took me a moment to absorb it. Not only could Kait not have told me about Roxanne's tattoo, that knowledge had not been in her memory bank when she died. For those who sought proof that those who die have on-going knowledge about events that occur on this earth plane after they've left it, that dream message would seem to provide that.

Meanwhile, the hits on Kait's website were rapidly increasing. My fellow writers were among the most frequent visitors, as the Mystery Writers of America had announced the URL in their newsletter.

Alec West, a writer in Washington State, became so incensed by the situation that he sent an impassioned e-mail to an assortment of New Mexico politicians.

"I am flabbergasted that the State of New Mexico hasn't stepped in officially to put this crime scandal to rest," he said.

No one responded.

Alec was not a man to take rejection lightly and contacted us for permission to organize a writers' e-mail campaign to bombard New Mexico officials with letters demanding that APD either re-open Kait's case or allow an outside agency to take over.

We gratefully accepted his offer, and Alec plunged into the

project with vigor. He suggested that we choose a symbolic day for this effort, such as Christmas, so people could "give Kait a present."

The image of Roxanne's heart leapt into my mind.

"I'd like it to be Valentine's Day," I said.

Alec set up a website that would allow participants to click on Kait's picture to send one message simultaneously to a number of public officials and to the media, with copies to Alec and us. We decided that the ideal time for the mailing would be February 13, after the politician/media types left their offices for the day. That way the mailings would filter in overnight, and when the recipients arrived at work on Valentine's Day they would be greeted by overflowing mailboxes.

With Alec handling the technical aspects of this venture, I devoted my own time to posting e-mail to writers around the country, inviting them to visit Kait's website and, if they felt comfortable doing so, participate in the campaign.

The day of February 13 seemed eighty hours long. As we inched our way through the final countdown, I was beset with the same sort of panic I used to feel when I gave one of our children a birthday party and none of the mothers bothered to RSVP. In effect, we were throwing a party for Kait, and I didn't think I could bear it if nobody came.

At precisely 6:00 p.m., Alec activated the website, and the floodgate flew open.

The first letter through set the mode for those that followed:

"A terrible crime has been committed in Albuquerque. The crime is not the murder of Kait Arquette, but the inadequate i.e. bungled job that the Albuquerque Police Department made of the investigation. It was criminal. As is necessary when crime is carried out, call in the

troops—in this case, the FEDS!!! It's time to police the police!!!"

We stayed up most of the night reading one supportive message after another, laughing and crying and cheering. Occasionally a familiar name would pop up to identify a known member of Kait's Army, but in general the letters were from strangers. The bottom line message was summed up in a one sentence e-mail from the editor of *Mysterious Galaxy*: "If Kait Arquette's concerned parents were able to gather the amount of information they have, surely the proper professionals can apply themselves to bringing her killers to justice."

The outpouring was so overwhelming that Alec was forced to close down the site before noon in response to complaints from recipients with overloaded servers. "What the hell are 5,000 God damned letters doing in my mail box?" one of them exploded.

The media latched onto the story with enthusiasm. An Associated Press article with the headline "E-MAIL CRUSADERS WANT TEEN'S MURDER SOLVED" began with the sentence, "It may seem like a strange plot twist—mystery writers banding together in cyberspace to pressure New Mexico officials to solve the murder of a teenager," and went on to describe Kait's website, "which questions the police investigation, accusing officers of failing to question important witnesses." APD responded to that with a statement that the department believed its investigation was complete.

The only person on the hit list who was willing to be interviewed was Department of Public Safety Secretary Darren White. "I have nothing but the utmost confidence in the homicide unit of the Albuquerque Police Department," said White, a former Albuquerque police sergeant.

By now killings by police officers in Albuquerque had reached such an all time high that the City Council commissioned an independent study "in the context of a serious and ongoing community crisis." The report confirmed that oversight mechanisms for the police department were not working.

"The number of shootings is extraordinarily high for a department of its size," one of the authors of the report told city councilors. He also disclosed the fact that the city set aside $4 million per year to settle claims against APD.

Since the largest portion of those settlements went to attorneys, it was easy to see why they might be reluctant to upset that lucrative apple cart.

Although the Valentine's Day campaign had no effect upon the people for whom it was intended, it did yank Kait's murder back into the public eye. *Inside Edition* filmed a segment about the case which included an interview with former DA, Bob Schwartz.

"I would categorize the police investigation as competent and thorough," he said, apparently forgetting his taped statement to me that the APD investigation was "sloppy and unskilled."

When the segment aired, Lieutenant Richard Tarango of the APD Violent Crimes Unit issued a statement to the media that APD's investigation had been solid.

"Nobody the Arquettes has brought to us has shown us a shred of evidence," he told reporters. "They have brought us *nothing.*"

That statement triggered a barrage of letters to the editor. Among those was one from Kait's therapist, saying, "I contacted the APD within days of Kait's murder and spoke to Detective Steven Gallegos. I reported information that seemed pertinent to her death. He declined to interview me."

Another outraged person to respond was Roxanne.

"I called Detective Steve Gallegos within days of the murder," she wrote. "I provided important information which to my understanding is not in the case file."

Those letters provided an impetus for other Albuquerque crime victims to get in touch with us. One was Nancy Grice, the nurse supervisor who had been on duty on Kait's ward the day that she died.

Now it was Nancy's own daughter who was dead.

"Melanie died in 1995," Nancy told me. "Her husband, Mark McCracken, a New Mexico State Police officer, said he found her unconscious on their bed. Instead of calling for an ambulance, he put her in the back of his car—ignoring his State Police car with lights, siren and radio, which was also in the driveway—drove onto the Indian reservation, and ran the car into a tree. The State Police told reporters that Melanie died in the car wreck. Mark said she died of leukemia. The autopsy showed no evidence of either."

Nancy requested an independent police investigation but was told there was no conflict of interest.

"No conflict of interest!" she exclaimed, her voice shaking with anger. "Mark's buddies were in charge of the investigation! I've appealed for help to every agency I can think of, and everybody's furious that I won't let this alone. I even received a call at work from a homicide detective, threatening to have me arrested for obstructing justice."

I hung up the phone and sat staring at my list of homicide survivors. These mothers had suffered the most excruciating loss any woman could experience and had hung in there to battle the System in behalf of their dead children. Every one of their names was engraved on my heart.

Betty's reading had said that, in a previous life, Michael Bush had been a "Tally Keeper."

"It was as if Michael will have been one to come along behind this family of warriors and take tally. This tally will sometimes have caused him great alarm."

As I scanned the names on the list of suspicious deaths—

Renee's son, Peter Klunck

Linda's son, Nathan Romero

Nancy's daughter, Melanie McCracken—

I realized with a shudder of horror that now it was I who had become the Tally Keeper.

CHAPTER THIRTEEN

A lbuquerque now had a new mayor, Jim Baca, who was doing his best to deal with the problems he'd fallen heir to. In response to newspaper headlines claiming, "THE CITIZENS OF ALBUQUERQUE ARE AFRAID OF THEIR COPS," Mayor Baca imported a new police chief from out of state to replace Joseph Polisar and was attempting to establish a citizen review board for police-misconduct cases.

"The police department has to be accountable to somebody besides themselves," Baca stated.

The police union was not happy with Mayor Baca's attitude.

The president of the Albuquerque Police Officers Association told the media,

"If he screws with us, we will do everything possible to defeat him in the next election."

Which they did.

The union strenuously objected to the idea of a review board. They contended that the Internal Affairs unit was more than sufficient to deal with charges of misconduct, despite the fact that for the past three years excessive force charges against police officers that were found to have merit had resulted in nothing more than written or oral reprimands.

"Letters of reprimand for beating the hell out of people is not

141

enough," said the director of Vecinos United, a group that had long decried continual civil and human rights violations by APD.

As the debate raged on, I received a call from Patti March, a founder of the New Mexico Survivors of Homicide.

Patti's son, Gary, had been murdered in Albuquerque in 1995.

"I read your book because I was told by a homicide detective that my family was a pain in the ass, just like the Arquettes," Patti told me. "We were doing the same things you did—talking to people the cops didn't talk to, printing flyers and trying to pressure the police to follow up on leads."

Patti told me that one of the mothers in the survivors group thought her son's murder might be linked in some way to Kait's. Of course, I phoned her.

Carmen Haar turned out to be the ultimate homicide survivor. Her son, Stephen, who had been shot to death in January 1998, was the *third* of Carmen's children to die a violent death.

"Steve had been estranged from the family because of his drug use," Carmen told me. "In the month before he was killed he tried to make amends. Steve told me twice, 'Mom, they're going to kill me.' I asked, 'Who is going to kill you?' He said, 'These are high profile people. It's best that you don't know.' I said, 'You're talking crazy. You think 'high profile people' kill people?' Steve said, 'They don't have to. Others do it for them.'"

"Do you know who killed Steve?" I asked her.

"A man named Travis Daley confessed to the shooting, but he claims self-defense, so the police won't charge him. How can it be self-defense when Steve was shot in the back? After Steve's death, I found a note in his pants pocket warning him about a contract that had been put out on him. I believe Steve was killed for the same reason Peter Klunck was—he knew too much about VIPs who were involved in the drug scene. Steve and Peter knew each other. Both did body work on cars. And both of them knew Matt Griffin."

When Pat ran the information about Steve Haar through her database, she did find a strange link to Kait's case. At the time of Steve's murder, he had lived at the same address as the witness who had told police he saw Kait followed from her apartment by a VW bug.

On August 4, 1998, the nurse, Nancy Grice, filed a federal civil rights suit against her former son-in-law, New Mexico State Police Sergeant Mark McCracken, and the state police chief. She accomplished that just one day before the statute of limitations ran out. "I couldn't get a lawyer, so I read some books and learned how to do it myself," she told me. Her suit was later amended to name other individual officers and the State Police in their official capacity. Nancy then petitioned the court to appoint an attorney for her and had Melanie's file submitted for review by a forensic expert.

Meanwhile, I had been contacted by yet another mother whose child had died in Albuquerque under suspicious circumstances. Jennifer Vihel's son, Josh, 16, had died of apparent alcohol poisoning at a party, but the fact that there were bruises on his body and money missing from his wallet caused his family to suspect foul play. Police claimed they were unable to question the party-givers, because they couldn't find their house. Josh's sister conducted her own investigation. She located the house with no problem and interviewed the neighbors, who told her the owners of the house threw frequent parties at which they charged cover fees and sold liquor and drugs to minors.

"One neighbor said she called in four complaints and no one ever did anything," Jennifer said.

I added *"Jennifer's son, Josh Vihel"* to my Tally Keeper notebook.

It had been a long time since I'd last consulted a psychic. In recent years my focus had been on practical matters—forensic data, crime scene evidence—things that could be used in court. Now, however, I found myself yearning for something more. I needed reassurance that there was still hope for all of us—that, as bad as things seemed, there was a Master Plan and we were part of it.

So I wrote to Betty Muench with yet another question:

"How is this going to end, or will there ever be an ending?"

Betty mailed me her reading:

"There will be this which will go beyond the enforcement officers of the law, for none locally can be trusted with this. But there will be other legal activity which will be connected to this. This will have to do with the infiltrating of certain groups, and this can only be done by men. This will have to be very assertive and aggressive and will ultimately require the use of the authorities in the manner of certain police actions. It will be like starting from the top and tracing all this information downward.

"There will be a final need to act, which will require the use of the highest form of policing, and that will be the federal level. There will be for Lois the continuing battle to put these pieces together, but there will come those with high integrity who can be trusted, and they will work with what she has already, and this will aid her greatly in the finding of those who will have knowledge of Kait's murder.

"Right now there is this group which is not understanding how

things operate and they will be making their own rules. When this will border on anarchy, they will fall, with truth coming out all around."

CHAPTER FOURTEEN

From the Tally Keeper's notebook:

New Case—Janie Phelps's son, Sal Martinez:
Sal arrived late at a bachelor party and was shot as he walked in the door. He was still alive when police got there, but the officers wouldn't perform CPR because they had forgotten their plastic mouthpieces. Police said they couldn't charge the admitted killer because he claimed self-defense, although Sal wasn't carrying a weapon, nor was anyone else at the party except the killer.

New Case—Valerie Duran's sister, Ramona Duran:
Ramona was found dead of a drug overdose in the apartment of two men with criminal records. There was a strong odor of gas, and Ramona had bruises on her arms. The first officer at the scene termed it "a suspicious death". A neighbor reported hearing a woman screaming. Ramona's family believes she was sedated with gas and forcibly injected with drugs. Ramona had told family members she feared for her life, because she had fingered VIPs in the drug trade.

Update—Nancy's Grice's daughter, Melanie McCracken:
Dr. John Smialek, expert witness in forensic pathology, issued a written opinion that Melanie died as a result of "homicidal suffoca-

tion." When it began to appear that the case might turn into a murder case, Nancy's court appointed attorney succumbed to pressure to settle out of court. The State Police then promoted Sergeant McCracken to the rank of lieutenant.

Update—*Carmen Haar's son, Stephen Haar:*
Police told reporters they were forwarding Stephen's case to the District Attorney. Months went by, and nothing happened. Carmen finally contacted the DA's office to ask why charges hadn't been filed. They told her APD had not sent them the case file.

In the fall of the year, a movie loosely based upon my novel, *I Know What You Did Last Summer,* opened in theaters around the country. This was my first box office movie and I was ecstatic until I settled into a theater seat and discovered that Hollywood had turned my story into a slasher film. The first thing I did after leaving the theater was phone our daughter, Kerry, and warn her not to let the grandchildren see it.

The positive side of this misadventure was that I had been paid for the film rights. We used part of that money to post a reward for new information about Kait's murder and donated the rest to help Pat turn her investigations agency non-profit so she could provide pro bono services to other crime victims.

We placed announcements about the reward in Albuquerque papers and mailed flyers to everyone remotely connected to the case. Among those were Dung and his girlfriend from Oregon.

The girlfriend reacted by calling the police. Since Pat's office number was on the flyer, she was the one police contacted with the harassment complaint. Pat explained that the reward offer was genuine and the girlfriend had not been specifically targeted, as we had mailed out over three hundred flyers. The officer seemed somewhat mollified but requested that Dung and his girlfriend be removed from our mailing list.

Then the girlfriend contacted Pat to accuse us of sending threatening letters and stalking her. Pat told her truthfully that we weren't doing either of those things.

"She said you sent Dung a video of one of Kait's birthday parties," Pat told me. "She found that very upsetting."

"I didn't send Dung any video!" I said. "Our family videos were stolen before we left Albuquerque."

"Well, I guess Dung's got one of them," Pat said.

Not long after that I received a frantic e-mail from Susan Smith. She, too, was receiving threatening messages in the mail and suspected that someone was stalking her.

We couldn't blame the two women for being frightened, since the incidents they described came right on the heels of our reward offer, and they were obvious candidates to claim that reward. Susan, who was the last person Kait spoke with before the shooting, and Dung's current girlfriend, who was regularly exposed to the same people and activities that Kait had been, might reasonably have been suspected of having access to the same information Kait did.

By now Pat had found two more witnesses, Bette Clark and Kathy Baca, the medical team who had transported Kait to the hospital. Locating them hadn't been easy, since Cop Number One had incorrectly identified a male ambulance team as first at the scene. The only reference to Bette and Kathy was in a report that they, themselves, had filed at the hospital. That's the first indication we had that it was more than a traffic accident."

"Cop Number One told me he couldn't take information from the man at the scene because he had to stay with the injured person," Pat said.

"He didn't stay with his victim," Bette said firmly. "There was nobody there."

"Cop Number Two said she couldn't take information because she was busy directing traffic."

"There were no cops at the scene when we got there," Bette reiterated. "No one was directing traffic. The place was deserted. We came with lights and sirens and we almost by-passed the scene because there was nobody there to wave us over."

Kathy was now a member of an emergency medical helicopter team, and Bette was a captain with the Albuquerque Fire Department.

Pat interviewed the women individually and then together, and their memories of that night were identical.

"What did you see when you got there?" Pat asked them.

"Nothing," Kathy told her. "I remember it was very dark. It was so quiet it was eerie."

"I remember that too," Bette said. "There was a red car up against a utility pole on the sidewalk. I don't know who could have made the call, because nobody was there."

"*Nobody was there!*" Pat exclaimed. "An off duty police detective stumbled onto the scene right after the shooting. He says he's the one who called for rescue."

"Then, where did he go?" Kathy asked her.

"A second, uniformed, female officer arrived at the scene in less than one minute," Pat continued. "She was dispatched to an accident without injuries and saw the detective standing behind Kait's car,

Rear end damage to Kait's car.

talking with a young man. She assumed that man was the driver of the red car, because no other cars were there. The detective told her, 'Don't worry, rescue is en route.' She said, 'Rescue? Why do we need rescue? He looks fine to me.' The detective said, 'No, we have a victim.'"

"Those people were there *before we were*?" Kathy exclaimed.

"Well, they left before we got there, then," Bette said.

"Then, who told you what happened to the victim?" Pat asked them.

"Nobody," Bette said. "We had to figure it out for ourselves. When we were removing the victim from the car, Kathy had her hands on the girl's head and felt the defects. That's the first indication we had that it was more than a traffic accident."

"Cop Number One told me he couldn't take information from the man at the scene because he had to stay with the injured person," Pat said.

"He didn't stay with his victim," Bette said firmly. "There was nobody there."

"Cop Number Two said she couldn't take information because she was busy directing traffic."

"There were no cops at the scene when we got there," Bette reiterated. "No one was directing traffic. The place was deserted. We came with lights and sirens and we almost by-passed the scene because there was nobody there to wave us over."

The medics then turned their attention to the scene photos.

"Is that new damage?" Kathy asked, indicating the car's rear bumper.

"Look right there!" Bette broke in before Pat could respond. "There's another good six inch intrusion in the *front* bumper! The only way you'd have that much intrusion into the pole is if there was acceleration or something pushed that car from the back."

"I don't understand why your names are not on the police reports," Pat said.

"It's probably because there was nobody there to identify us," Bette speculated.

Pat transcribed the interviews and both women signed affidavits.

It was one more piece in a jigsaw puzzle created by a madman.

There were nights when I lay in bed, too emotionally exhausted to fall asleep, and tried to recall what it had been like to live in an orderly world. I had once been a woman who was seemingly blessed with everything—good health, a happy marriage, five children, a career and a stimulating social life. If anyone had suggested that a day might come when I would have only four children, when I couldn't care less about writing, when my closest friends would be private

LOIS DUNCAN

investigators, psychic detectives, and the families of murder victims, I would have considered them insane.

Eventually such thoughts would become blurry and start running together and I would slide into sleep, but always now it was a fitful sleep, racked by disturbing dreams. Occasionally one of those dreams would stand out from the others in ways that made me wonder if it was more than a dream. The colors were more vivid, the sounds and aromas were clearer, and many times those dreams contained printed text like the *"Katie sat down and read a magazine"* message in my dream about Roxanne's heart tattoo.

One night I dreamed that I was looking at a children's picture book. There was an illustration of a small car with a little slip of paper floating toward the ground as if it had been dropped from the driver's side window. Beneath that picture ran a line of text—*"If only they knew about the ticket it would explain a lot to them."* As I stared at that image, it was abruptly replaced by a picture of a parking lot filled with cars. Near the front, there was a red Ford Tempo. Beneath that picture the text said, *"Look for the BLUE CAR!"* In my dream I started scanning the rows of cars in search of a blue one but couldn't find one. Then, suddenly, a large car pulled out from behind the small red car. It was a police car.

I awoke with my heart pounding and a strong feeling that this was indeed a message. Psychics had told us that Kait's car was stationery when she was shot, and the accuracy of the shooting supported that theory. Our question had always been, what could have caused her to stop where there was no stop sign or traffic light? My dream contained a possible answer—*Kait would have stopped if she had been pulled over by a police car!*

As a writer by trade I am practiced in creating scenes. This one

152

comes without effort as if it's a video playing in my head. A police car materializes behind Kait with its lights flashing. Kait, who is no stranger to traffic tickets, starts to slow down. The police car then rams her car, damaging the bumper and side panel and propelling it across the median and up onto the opposite curb. Kait sits there, trapped and terrified, hemmed in on all sides as predators congregate around her like a pack of wolves. I build my cast of characters, playing no favorites. An Quoc Le is at the forefront, with Dung and Khanh Pham right behind him. Paul Apodaca is there with his brother, Mark, and their drug dealer, Lee. Miguel Garcia and Juve Escobedo are there, accompanied by Marty Martinez, who carefully sets his beer can down on the curb, intending to retrieve it later. There is no record of a traffic ticket, because the driver of the police car doesn't issue one. The imaginary traffic violation was a pretext for stopping Kait. This is a phantom ticket, existing only in her mind in her final moments of consciousness.

It is Kait's ticket to the After World.

I knew that Don and Pat would have a hard time accepting that scenario, so I didn't mention it. But I recorded the dream in my journal against a day when it would either be proved or disproved.

I didn't expect that day to come as soon as it did.

I had become accustomed to receiving e-mail from visitors to Kait's Web page, so I wasn't surprised to find a message with the subject line, "Kait," in my inbox:

I was in Albuquerque for a wedding back in 1989 and was just up the street from where it happened. We passed by it on our way to the motel. I saw the car and Kait. I can't believe that this has gone unsolved this long.

May God be with you.
Carolyn

I started to respond with a routine "Thank you for caring," and then did a double take. *"I saw the car and Kait."* How could this woman have seen Kait? Both Cop Number One and Cop Number Two had reported finding Kait prone across both bucket seats with her head against the passenger door.

I sent Carolyn an e-mail asking her to describe the scene. Were there other cars there? Were police directing traffic? Had a crowd gathered?

"Your memories could be very helpful," I told her.

"In 1989, I was twenty-three," Carolyn responded. "I had driven to Albuquerque from out-of-state to attend a wedding. We went out to eat around 9:00 p.m. to some steak-type restaurant and were going back to our motel. I remember a car being up on the sidewalk and a girl's bloody head. A cop car was there and a cop. I don't remember anyone directing traffic. My Mom remembers me coming home from the wedding and telling her that I had seen the car and Kait."

I asked Carolyn if she would be willing to talk with our investigator. She said sure, but she didn't think she had anything of value to contribute. All she had seen was Kait in her car and a police officer standing next to her.

Carolyn told Pat the same story but provided more details.

"She and other people from the wedding party were driving from the restaurant to their motel," Pat told me. "Carolyn was in the backseat, looking out the side window, and noticed a car up on the sidewalk. She says the driver's door was open and she could see a blond girl with bloody hair. A police officer was standing next to the driver's door. She said it looked like he had just opened it to check on the girl and was glancing to the West as if expecting someone. Carolyn assumed he was waiting for an ambulance. She remembers being aware that there was no need to stop because the police were already there. It wasn't until the next day when she saw the story on the news that she realized that what she'd thought was a car accident had been a shooting."

"The officer might have been Cop Number One," I suggested.

"Not possible," Pat said. "He was dressed in street clothes and driving an unmarked car. Besides, he said he never went to the driver's side. And when Carolyn passed the scene, Kait was still upright. Perhaps she toppled over because the uniformed officer inadvertently pushed her while feeling for a pulse."

"Did Carolyn come across to you as credible?" I asked.

"She sounded open and unsophisticated, and she didn't seem to have an agenda," Pat said. "I can't envision a situation that would cause her to make up something like this. I've spoken to the parents of the bride, and they confirm the fact that Carolyn came to Albuquerque to attend the wedding and was staying at a motel only blocks from the scene. Carolyn says it was almost eleven when they left the restaurant—the staff was getting ready to close up—so the timing is right."

She paused and then continued, "If what Carolyn says is accurate, a police officer may have been at the scene when Kait was murdered."

CHAPTER FIFTEEN

The new police chief, Gerald Galvin, seemed to be doing his best to deal with the problems Mayor Baca had imported him to rectify, but he was in a difficult position. The former police chief, Joseph Polisar, had enjoyed the support of the police union, while Galvin, as an out-of-state replacement, was regarded with suspicion by many of his officers. That hostility was aggravated by Galvin's public support for the concept of a citizen review board.

"I will not tolerate police misconduct," Galvin stated.

Chief Galvin was also attempting to initiate the formation of a Cold Case Unit to investigate old unsolved cases. When we asked him if Kait's case could be one of those, he assured us that the Cold Case detectives would be very open to reviewing our new information with an eye toward possibly reactivating the case.

However, when Pat submitted an overview of her investigation, the supervisor of the Cold Case Unit became hostile.

"My detectives assure me there are no suspects other than the men they arrested," she told Pat. She went on to state that, because my book had maligned "an impeccable department," APD would not accept any information from us or our representatives. They wouldn't even give credence to a statement by the former medic, Bette Clark, who recently had been named Chief of the Bernalillo County Fire Department.

When we posted that on Kait's website, the police were incensed. "I dispute the allegations that we refused to investigate!" an APD spokesperson told reporters. "If information comes to us, we'll act on it, because *that's what we do!*"

The Police Oversight Commission that Chief Galvin had supported turned out to be a disappointment. Though fine in theory, it lacked teeth. The commission was hampered in their efforts to obtain information about police transgressions by the fact that APD was not obligated to turn over their reports. Although citizens could appeal to the commission, the police chief did not have to act on the commission's recommendations, and no officer named in a citizen complaint had ever shown up for a hearing.

"We have been stonewalled," the commission chairman told the media.

Meanwhile, the Tally Keeper's notebook was rapidly filling:

New Case*–Arry Frank's sister, Stephane Murphey:*
Stephane was sexually assaulted and strangled in Rio Rancho, just outside of Albuquerque. Her decomposed body was found four days later in her car.

Police processed the scene as a burglary and compromised much of the evidence by allowing outsiders to walk around in Stephane's house before they took fingerprints. They also resisted submitting DNA evidence to the crime lab. The lead detective told the family he was "stumped" and had nothing more to investigate.

Update*–Nancy Grice's daughter, Melanie McCracken:*
NBC Dateline took an interest in Melanie's case and set up a meet-

ing with a magistrate judge. "When the producer attempted to meet with the judge, two state cop cars blocked the road and turned their lights in her face," Nancy said. "She was so scared that she filed a report with her legal department."

The producer then set up an interview with the former head of an ambulance service about numerous 911 calls allegedly made from the McCracken home. That interview didn't take place because the witness was found hanged in his garage on the day before the scheduled interview. (An alleged suicide).

New Case—*Bill Houston's daughter, Stephanie Houston:*
Stephanie died when her boyfriend ran her over with his truck after he saw her dancing with another man. The Medical Examiner urged that Stephanie's death be investigated as a homicide. The scene investigator, Mark McCracken, (the same "Mark McCracken" who was under investigation for the suspicious death of his wife, Melanie), told the media that his department had fully investigated and Stephanie had caused her own death because she was falling-down drunk. In truth, they had questioned no witnesses, done no reconstruction, and the toxicology test showed Stephanie had very little alcohol in her system.

It didn't seem possible that the world could contain so much agony. The cases piling up in my notebook were featured briefly in local newspapers and within a few days were replaced by accounts of fresh atrocities. In our own case, at least, I'd been able to get a book published, but most families in our position weren't so fortunate. After the first rush of sympathy, even personal friends turned away from them, made uncomfortable by what they perceived as obsessive complaints about the way the cases were being mishandled.

An article in the *Albuquerque Tribune* quoted the new mayor, Martin Chavez, as stating, "We are on the verge of having one of the best police departments in the country." People desperately wanted to believe that.

A mother named Rosemary Sherman didn't think that applied to the Sheriff's Department. Rosemary's son, John, had been found, slashed and stabbed to death in his van just outside of Albuquerque.

"In addition to the stab wounds, Johnny's throat had been cut and his teeth knocked out," Rosemary told me. "Sheriff's deputies did no investigation. They just said, 'It's a suicide. Bag the body and let's go home.'

"John's van was not processed for prints or DNA evidence. The alleged weapon, a razor, was not seized as evidence. When I asked the lead detective about that, he said, 'It was in a pool of blood, so I left it in the van.' I requested that the razor be examined by a forensic expert to determine if it really was the weapon that slashed my son's body. The detective didn't want to do that. I took the autopsy report and the scene photos to a former head of forensics at the Menninger Clinic. He told me, 'This wasn't just murder, this was over-kill.'

"I also met with an FBI agent, who is a very nice guy. He indicated that in his opinion something stunk, but he told me errors in handling of an investigation don't fall under federal civil rights laws. In other words, the FBI can't step into the case unless I can prove *malfeasance*. It's not enough to show the police didn't do their job, I have to prove that they acted out of malice! How can I possibly prove what was in their heads?"

"You're not alone," I told her. "We're in the same position, and so are a lot of others."

"Perhaps we could unite," Rosemary said. "If we pooled our

LOIS DUNCAN

information about mishandled cases it might start forming a pattern. Maybe we could find some way to use that to bring the attention of the citizens of our state, or maybe even the entire nation,
to the problems with law enforcement in this country." She paused
and then added wistfully, "I know that's just a pipe dream. We could
never find enough families with the courage to do that."

"I don't know about that," I said thoughtfully as I glanced across
my desk at the Tally Keeper's notebook.

We launched our Real Crimes website in 1998. A philanthropic
friend, Tom Arriola, sponsored it, linking it to his own site. I interviewed the families and helped them word their stories, and Don
linked their allegations to documentation such as autopsy reports,
depositions and scene photos.

It didn't take long for people to discover the site, and people
outside of New Mexico began to submit their own stories. We ex-
panded the site to include those, although the preponderance of
cases was still from New Mexico. Tom created message boards so
visitors could discuss the cases. Among the most vocal were private
investigators, forensic experts, police officers and attorneys, who
leapt upon the discrepancies between information in police reports
and the visual evidence in scene photos.

One out-of-state cop's knee jerk reaction to Kait's case was, "To
assume that any conspiracy, let alone a police conspiracy, is at hand
is pretty much pushing the envelope of common sense."

But after viewing the photos from the crime scene, he reversed
his opinion:

"Okay, I'm now a believer," he posted. "Judging from the picture
of the bullet hole in Kait's car, I would have to say that she was run

160

off the road and the killer exited his vehicle and fired the shots into her car. This is based on the height of the bullet hole in the door-frame and the apparent angle of strike."

Disgruntled ex-wives and ex-girlfriends of witnesses, suspects and police officers posted information that they'd obtained during pillow talk. There was no way to know how much of their input was valid, but Pat did her best to try to verify it.

The most heartbreaking message was from Bill Houston, the father of Stephanie Houston, the woman who was run over by her jealous boyfriend.

"I hate to bother you again," Bill said apologetically. *"But do you have a limit on how many cases you post per family? Our younger daughter, Crystal, has now been murdered."*

Back in Albuquerque, Pat Caristo was busy. Requests for pro bono services had become too overwhelming for her small agency to handle. She was even receiving secret requests from members of law enforcement asking for help with cases that had been mishandled by their own departments.

To enlarge her workforce, Pat created an internship program in which graduates of the course in private investigation that she taught at the University of New Mexico could obtain the on-the-job experience they needed for certification by working as apprentices. Kait's case was the focus of many of their training sessions.

One subject of particular interest to the interns was the body shop on Arno. The fact that the shop not only was frequented by Vietnamese, but was a location where drugs were dealt and rogue cops hung out, was intriguing to this group of young crime-solvers.

One of them even wanted to apply for a job there. Pat quickly vetoed that suggestion.

Pat drove past the shop on almost a daily basis, as it was located between her office and the Post Office. Sometimes she was startled to see a limousine parked there. Then she started noticing some changes in activity, such as the positioning of cars inside the fenced area at the back, which made it difficult for her to read their license plates.

One day, when she drove past, the building was a skeleton. It had been destroyed in a fire.

Pat called the foundation that leased out the property and obtained permission to visit the burned out building and recover any unclaimed documents that had survived the fire. She was told she had better move quickly as the property had been sold and the new owners soon would be tearing down the remains of the building.

The maintenance man used his keys to open the iron gate, and Pat and her interns finally had access to what remained of the hub of illegal activity that all of us had wondered about for so long. They entered the building from the back, stepping carefully over fallen beams and the blackened remnants of what once had been furniture. They discovered the building was divided into three major areas—the south end that had contained the business offices, which was where the fire had started; the middle working area for vehicle repair; and the north end, where the manager had apparently run a second business operation. A kitchen area and a bathroom were located in the middle section of the building. The second floor had collapsed in the fire, so they were unable to determine if there had been an upper level living area that might have been used for parties.

In the ghostly silence of the building, Pat couldn't help but recall the reading Betty Muench had done in response to that particular street address:

"During the time of Kait's involvement there was attention placed on this address by many sources. Some of those will be listed, but this also was under the scrutiny of federal authorities, who were not consulted during the investigation of Kait's murder.

"Kait, herself, did not visit this place in person, but both before and after her death, those in attendance will have on various occasions spoken her name here. Dung's energy is felt here because of his anger, both before and after Kait's death. He was in a rage in this place. The Hispanic suspect, Juve Escobedo, was here also. This was after the death of Kait. He enters midst much attention with a sense of expectancy. He is to receive something."

Pat forced the psychic images out of her mind and focused her full attention on the job at hand. She and her interns conducted a walk-through of the building, collecting papers, checks, forms, and ledger pages that were scattered among the ashes. Then, they returned to Pat's office to do an inventory.

The majority of the material they retrieved was dated in the mid-to-late 1980s. That included a series of checks, signed by the owner's girlfriend, who also had worked as his bookkeeper. This was the same woman who had told investigator, Roy Nolan, that she and the owner had been introduced to Kait at a disco, when Kait was there with a woman who fit the description of Susan Smith.

One check, dated May 24, 1986, was made out to "Susan Gonzales"* in a handwriting that was different from the bookkeeper's handwriting. On the back of that check was written "Smith Deposit." The check was stamped for deposit in an out-of-state bank.

"We have something here that we need to look into," Pat said.

When her students regarded her blankly, she continued, "'Susan Smith' is the name of the friend Kait visited on the night of the murder. Susan's maiden name was 'Gonzales.' Several months after this check was written, Susan married a man named 'Smith.' The bank where this check was deposited is in the town where the couple lived at that time. It's possible this is a coincidence. But if it isn't, that would mean that Kait's new friend, who routed her down Lomas that night, received a check from people linked to this business three years before she moved to Albuquerque. I've no idea what the significance of this may be, but we need to find out whether the person who received this check is *our* 'Susan Gonzales Smith.'"

"How do we do that?" one of the interns asked.

"We need to locate the employee who wrote the check," Pat said. "The owner of the shop is now deceased. Your assignment is to track down his employee-girlfriend."

The interns set out eagerly on their mission, but the challenge was more than they could handle. The bookkeeper had married, divorced, remarried, and divorced again, and was listed in public records under four different names. Following her court history of fraud, forgery, and embezzlement, the interns tracked her progress as she racked up residences in ten towns in two different states. Then the trail ran out.

One more lead down the drain.

However, Pat was able to locate and interview Susan Smith's best friend, the woman Susan had trusted to forward her tax statements. That friend told Pat that she hadn't met Kait in person, but Susan had talked a lot about her. The friend said, according to Susan, a few days prior to the murder, Kait had overheard Dung screaming on the phone. She heard enough to get the gist of the conversation and had told Dung, "I know what you guys are up to, and I don't want to get involved."

Dung had responded, "Too late. You're already involved."

"Involved in what?" Pat asked.

Susan's friend became nervous and refused to say anything more.

In 2003, the Bernalillo County Sheriff's Department formed its own Cold Case Unit. The officers who came out of retirement to man the unit had impressive track records and were actively solving old cases.

One detective, a former FBI agent, had spent forty-seven years in law enforcement. In a newspaper interview, Bernalillo County Sheriff Darren White described him as "no frills—100 percent cop—a legend."

Although the Sheriff's Department didn't have jurisdiction over Kait's case, Pat, who had met the detective socially, decided there was nothing to lose by requesting his unofficial take on the physical evidence. He agreed to review the scene materials, so Pat sent him the APD field and forensic reports and the scene photos.

The detective responded with his written opinion:

1) This was not a random drive-by shooting.

2) The shooting occurred after Kaitlyn's vehicle struck the utility pole.

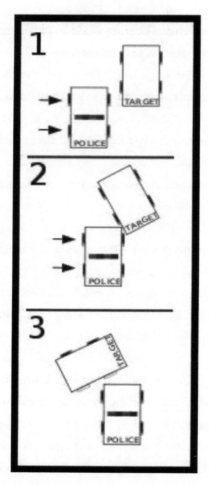

PIT Technique for forcing car off the road.

3) The accuracy of the shots suggests they were fired at a very close range at a non-moving target.

4) Had the shooting taken place while the victim's car was in motion, it would have veered to the right of the roadway due to the left-to-right camber of the pavement. Also, the victim's falling to the right would have turned the steering wheel in that direction if she was grasping the steering wheel at the time of shooting.

5) Damage to the left end of the rear bumper suggests the rear of her vehicle was struck and pushed to the right by a second vehicle which veered her car across the median and into the utility pole.

6) This shooting was intentional and Ms. Arquette was the specific target.

From an Internet search I learned that the method of tactical ramming described in Point # Five is called the "PIT Technique" and is widely used by police to force a car off the road. I was able to find a diagram that depicted the process. It meshed precisely with the damage to Kait's rear bumper.

This report from a highly respected member of law enforcement supported our suspicions, but what could we do with it? The APD Cold Case Unit had disbanded, and no other agency had the authority to follow up on this.

But one thing I did now have was an interpretation of the odd postscript that Kait had tacked onto one of Betty's early readings: *"Mom, I love you. Look out for the walker, the innocent walker, who does more than walk."*

Apparently Kait had been shot by someone on foot.

By now, the families who posted their stories on our website had begun to network among themselves, sharing information and occasionally establishing links between what initially appeared to be unrelated cases. The families of twenty-four New Mexico murder victims became so closely united that they held their own press conference in Albuquerque to demand the creation of a New Mexico Bureau of Investigation with jurisdiction to investigate cold cases throughout the state and to investigate any case in which there was a conflict of interest involving the investigating agency and the victim or the suspect. The families' stories cited instances of alleged malfeasance involving nine New Mexico law enforcement agencies.

Despite the fact that she'd broken a leg and was in a wheelchair, Rosemary Sherman flew to Albuquerque from her home in California to keynote the conference. Rosemary described her meeting with the new Sandoval County sheriff, who had promised to reopen her son's case. "When the sheriff pulled John's case file to prepare for our meeting yesterday, he discovered that the previous sheriff had shredded its contents," she said. "There is nothing left but a partial autopsy report."

The press conference received extensive coverage by the media, followed by a flurry of horrified letters to local newspapers. One week later, it was as if the event never happened. It was yesterday's news.

However, the website continued to elicit new information in regard to the top echelon of the New Mexico drug scene:

One person wrote: *"This is in response to the psychic's description of the house in the mountains where Kait Arquette saw a VIP buy drugs. I know all about those homes and what they are used for. A man I used to do business with in New Mexico got involved with a drug cartel. He purchased a number of homes, some with airstrips. That's how the cartel laundered money. Some of those homes were mansions worth millions of dollars. Rarely did anyone live in them. Occasionally they would be used for visitors of the cartel or other drug transactions."*

So many people seemed to have first hand knowledge about VIPs who controlled the New Mexico drug scene, yet no one was willing to speak out. And with good reason. There was no way to know whom to trust.

CHAPTER SIXTEEN

Although the Real Crimes site had not yet produced any miracles, it was serving the purpose for which it was created–bringing allegations of mishandled cases to the attention of the public. A number of reporters and TV producers were using the site as a resource, and an investigative Internet newspaper was running a series of articles titled "Corruption in New Mexico." Several of our cases were also subjects of books.

From the Tally Keeper's notebook:

Update—Nancy Grice's daughter, Melanie McCracken:
Melanie's case was featured on NBC Dateline, earning them the Edward R. Murrow Award for investigative reporting.

Update—Arry Frank's sister, Stephane Murphey:
Thanks to on-going pressure from a reporter, the Rio Rancho Department of Public Safety finally agreed to submit DNA evidence from under Stephane's fingernails to CODIS (Combined DNA Index System Program). The DNA matched that of a prison inmate, David Bologh, who had been a neighbor of Stephane's. Bologh was arraigned on charges of murder, kidnapping, aggravated burglary, auto theft and tampering with evidence.

Update—*Bill Houston's daughter, Stephanie Houston:*

After nearly four years, Bill and his private investigator were finally able to convince the district attorney to reopen Stephanie's case. A grand jury indicted her boyfriend, Patrick Murillo, on a vehicular homicide charge.

No, the Red Sea, (or, more aptly, "The Blue Sea"), had not parted, but some waves had been created. The voices of the twenty-four families who spoke out at the Albuquerque press conference had been twenty-four times louder than the voice of one family alone.

In June 2004, I was invited to speak at a convention of the New Mexico Survivors of Homicide. It was a moving experience to finally meet in person some of the families that I had come to feel so close to through e-mail and phone conversations.

Following my opening talk, a panel of judges entertained questions from the audience. As I studied the names in the program, I realized there had been a substitution. The Chief Judge of the judicial district that covered all of Bernalillo County was missing from the line-up.

"Where's the star of the panel?" I whispered to the woman seated next to me.

She turned to regard me with surprise. "You mean you haven't heard?"

"Heard what?" I asked.

"He's been arrested. He and a lady friend were stopped when they tried to avoid a DWI checkpoint. They'd apparently come from a party. The judge had cocaine on the crotch of his pants and a bindle of it in his lap. He's been charged with drug possession and tampering with evidence."

"Where was the party?" I asked.

"Who cares?" the woman said. "He was out with his friends snorting coke. Isn't that enough?"

No, it's not enough, I thought, although I didn't say it aloud. If this renowned judge was doing drugs at a party, there must have been other well-connected people in attendance.

I leaned forward and tapped the shoulder of a reporter in the row in front of me.

"Who does the judge who got arrested hang out with?" I asked her.

"There's a clique," she told me. "It's tight and goes back a long way. Politicians and well known business people." She paused and, then, as she realized where our conversation was headed, added hastily, "Of course, he has other friends too. He's a popular man."

There were immediate calls for the judge's removal from the bench. After issuing a statement of apology to his family and the public, he was whisked away to the Betty Ford Clinic in California. Protesters lined up outside the courthouse, furious that the judge remained eligible for retirement benefits because he'd submitted his resignation before he could be suspended. One outraged woman stood sweltering in the 95 degree heat, waving a sign that read, "Who's your dealer, Judge?"

Legislators expressed their concern that "one sad, isolated incident" might undermine the integrity of the System in the eyes of the public.

But, as it turned out, it was not one isolated incident.

Several days after the judge's arrest, an investigative reporter exploded a TV news story that revealed that the judge had a lengthy history of using illegal drugs. The story was based upon information in a long-buried narcotics report that alleged that the judge's cocaine use had been known to law enforcement for at least eight years, along with the names of other socially prominent drug users.

The judge's name appeared four times in the forty-eight-page report, which documented a Department of Public Safety investigation to pinpoint participants in New Mexico's multi-million dollar drug trafficking business.

Bernalillo County Sheriff Darren White, who had been the DPS secretary at the time the report was written, denied knowing anything about it.

The TV station stood by their story.

As the conflict continued, more information surfaced. The report had, indeed, been prepared by a DPS agent, who was assigned as the state's representative to an Organized Crime and Drug Enforcement Task Force. The document detailed drug smuggling and money laundering in New Mexico that spanned twenty years, along with a list of participants that—according to the privileged few who had seen the report—read like a "Who's Who" of the New Mexico drug underworld, with judges, lawyers, politicians, sports celebrities and prominent businessmen listed right alongside the state's narcotics kingpins.

Because no charges had been brought against any of those people, their names could not be released.

The Judicial Standards Commission obtained a copy of the report, and David Iglesias, US Attorney for New Mexico, was interviewed on television.

Reporter: *Important document?*
Iglesias: *Absolutely!*

Reporter: *Eye opener?*

Iglesias: *A page-turner. I couldn't put it down.*

Governor Bill Richardson asked the state Judicial Standards Commission to initiate an investigation.

The judge's attorney was adamantly against such a probe.

"That's the kind of crap that can ruin people's lives," he said.

People's lives have already been ruined! I longed to scream at him. The drug activities of the people on that VIP list dated back to before Kait's murder. A limousine driver told investigators that, in the 1980s, he transported the judge and two prominent attorneys to Santa Fe to meet with legislators at a bar, and the judge and his associates used cocaine throughout the trip. It stood to reason that the legislators they were planning to spend the evening with would have been involved in the same activity. *Who were they?*

Three psychics, from different areas of the country, had given almost identical responses to our question, "Who was the VIP Kait saw involved in a drug transaction?" Those descriptions formed a thumbnail sketch that I thought I might recognize if I could compare it to names of the people in the narcotics report.[10]

I did everything I could to get a list of the names, but even my reporter friends couldn't get access to them. Unless the VIPs were careless enough to be caught with cocaine in their crotches their identities would forever be protected.

When the (now former) judge returned from rehab, he pleaded guilty to DWI and possession of cocaine. He was sentenced to a year's probation and two days of house arrest and given a conditional discharge on the drug charge, so the felony conviction would eventually be removed from his record. His lady friend also pleaded guilty and received the same "punishment." By entering guilty pleas, they avoided trial, which meant they never would be forced to disclose where they had been that night or identify their drug suppliers.

Years were passing, and Don and I were growing old. We kept ourselves busy adding cases to the ever-expanding Real Crimes site and doing volunteer work. We had developed a casual social life on the Outer Banks, but we missed the longtime friendships we'd enjoyed in New Mexico. Most of all, we missed our children. With the loss of Kait, the family unit had fragmented, and our surviving children were scattered all over the country. We visited them, of course, and they visited each other, but the solid structure of "Family" no longer existed and our lives felt empty without it.

Then, one day, when I was feeling particularly downhearted, Pat called with some up-lifting news.

"Remember the detective with the Bernalillo County Cold Case Squad, who was convinced Kait was forced off the road and then shot?" she said. "Well, I ran into him and his wife last night at a barbecue, and he told me he's submitted his findings to the APD Cold Case Unit."

"I thought that unit had folded!" I exclaimed in surprise.

"It had, but it's now been resurrected," Pat told me. "The new lead detective is said to be honest and dedicated. This could be the break we've been praying for!"

The *Albuquerque Tribune* ran a lengthy article about the new APD Cold Case Unit, stating that the lead detective was "the first Albuquerque Police Department agent to take seriously the reams of information acquired by the family in the Kaitlyn Arquette case."

"I believe the evidence is strong, very strong," the detective was quoted as saying. "The family's private investigator and I have agreed to sit down together. There's so much more we can do now that we couldn't years ago. That's what's really going to solve these cases—forensic science."

When Pat met with the detective she was favorably impressed. She described him as friendly and accessible and interested in reviewing her information as long as it didn't implicate the Vietnamese.

"The homicide detectives have assured him they thoroughly investigated the Vietnamese angle and there's nothing to it," Pat said. "They've told him your book is fiction, so he won't even read it. I assured him I'm not convinced that the Vietnamese killed Kait. They're a bunch of crooks and I feel sure they were somehow connected, but I'm thinking now that somebody else did the shooting."

"Maybe so," I conceded. "But Dung or his friends must have been there. How else could he have known about it three hours before he was told?"

"The detective said the case can't be prosecuted, no matter how strong the evidence, because the statute of limitations has run out," Pat said. "I told him the most important thing is to uncover the truth so the family can have closure."

"I thought there was no statute of limitations on murder!"

"That's true today, but not in 1989," Pat said. "Back then, the statute of limitations on murder in New Mexico was fifteen years. That law has since been changed, but the detective tells me it's not retroactive."

"You mean, if somebody came forward tomorrow and confessed to the murder, he wouldn't be charged?" I asked incredulously.

"Probably not," Pat said.

When the story about the detective's willingness to work on Kait's case appeared in the paper, we received an anonymous e-mail that contained a veiled threat to other members of our family. Then we began to be told things that seemed deliberately designed to send us off on tangents. Members of law enforcement seemed suddenly to be confiding inside information about Kait's case to everybody they met, and those people were helpfully passing those statements on to us: (1) Kait had been having an affair with Cop Number One and he killed her because she was becoming too possessive; (2) Kait was an APD snitch and was killed in a drug sting; (3) Kait was shot as a message to me that people didn't like my books; (4) and, of course, the old standby—Kait was the victim of a car-jacking.

We didn't believe any of those statements, yet we couldn't arbitrarily dismiss them on the very slim chance that one might actually be accurate. So hours of our time and Pat's were spent checking out leads, all of which proved to be dead ends.

Pat continued to meet with the detective, but their conferences were turning out to be less productive than we'd hoped.

"He has total faith in the homicide department," Pat told us. "He acknowledges there were some problems with the investigation, but he's certain those weren't intentional."

"What does he have to say about the fact that no one was there when the ambulance arrived?"

"Police reports don't support that, so he doesn't believe it."

"But the police reports are filled with misinformation!"

"He doesn't think that way, and that's understandable. His launching pad is the information in the case file. If he questions that, he'll have no foundation to build on. He's not out to reinvent the wheel, just to keep it rolling. Homicide detectives have assured him the Hispanic suspects killed Kait, so his goal is to get information to support that scenario."

The detective then received a startling new lead. An alleged eyewitness had resurfaced with information that could nail Miguel Garcia. The detective would not tell Pat the identity of this witness, but he did reveal that she was female and said he was working hard to gain her confidence.

"It sounds like that's going to keep him busy," Don commented. "Too busy, I guess, to follow up on any of the other stuff."

To us it seemed oddly coincidental that this eyewitness would suddenly pop up after fifteen years. The term "resurfaced" implied she was already known. If her information was so important and incriminating, why had Bob Schwartz decided not to prosecute? The whole situation felt suspect, and we couldn't help wondering if this honest detective—an obvious threat to a cover-up—had been served up a manufactured witness in a deliberate attempt to divert his attention from Pat's information. If so, there had to be some way to get him re-focused.

"I've heard there's now an excellent ballistics expert at APD," I said. "Perhaps the detective would be willing to ask him to compare the partial bullet from the door frame with the minute bullet fragments from Kait's head. He did say forensic science was the key to solving cases."

"If bullet fragments are incriminating evidence, what makes you think they still exist?" Don asked doubtfully.

"They *have* to exist," I insisted. "They were checked into evidence. All the things in the evidence room are protected."

The irony of that statement became apparent when we pulled up the on-line edition of the *Albuquerque Journal* and were faced with a banner headline:

CLEANUP DESTROYED APD EVIDENCE

According to the article, evidence from hundreds of cases, most of them drug related, had been destroyed at the Albuquerque Police Department during the cleanup of hazardous chemicals, which had been spilled on evidence bags.

Apparently, nothing in the evidence room was protected.

CHAPTER SEVENTEEN

The chemical spill was the tip of the iceberg.

The Attorney General's Office received an anonymous letter claiming that for many years police employees had been stealing huge amounts of cash, drugs, guns and other valuable items from the evidence room and APD management had covered that up.

The current police chief was quick to deny the accusation. To reinforce that denial, he invited the media to tour the evidence room.

(Courtesy: Albuquerque Journal)

During the tour, Sergeant Cynthia Orr seemed reluctant to answer questions and asked her supervisor if she had permission to speak freely. He assured her that the department wanted them to be open and honest, so Sergeant Orr invited a reporter into her office and agreed to be recorded.

The sergeant told the reporter that the police chief had lied to the public and had failed to act despite repeated warnings of evidence theft. Orr said that she, personally, had identified two individuals who were stealing in the evidence room, but the chief had allowed them to continue to work there. She went on to describe how officers under criminal investigation were allowed to work in the evidence room where they were free to tamper with the evidence in their own cases. Orr said she was told not to send reports about missing evidence to the records division because the Top Brass didn't want it to become public record that items were missing.

"Am I implicating the chief in assisting in this cover-up? Absolutely," Orr said. "Do I know this is a dangerous accusation to make? Absolutely. But I know this is something that needs to be done."

USA Today picked up the story and it went viral. "The APD Evidence Room Scandal," as it came to be known, continued to accelerate as additional whistle-blowers gained the courage to come forward. The list of valuable property that had been sold at auction or "taken to the dump," (which we assumed meant employees took it home with them), grew longer and longer. An example of such items was a $15,000 plasma television set, which was seized as evidence in a white-collar crime investigation and was supposed to be returned to the owner after the trial. Evidence room personnel said they "took the TV to the dump" because it had a crack in it.

Keep Mouths Shut or Else

PAT VASQUEZ-CUNNINGHAM/JOURNAL

Albuquerque Police Lieutenant Joseph Byers taped Deputy Police Chief Paul Chavez telling a March 17 assembly of Field Service Bureau lieutenants that officers who talked to the media would face consequences.

(Courtesy: Albuquerque Journal)

There was instant retaliation against the whistleblowers. A captain, who had reported the damage from the chemical spill, was asked to turn in her badge, gun and squad car. A different captain, who had ordered an investigation into high-ranking members of the police department, was punished by having the Internal Affairs division taken away from his command. At two citywide meetings, attended by hundreds of officers who were required to be there, deputy chiefs encouraged them to be "angry and repulsed" by Sergeant Orr for breaking the code of silence.

In a furious tirade, filled with profanity, one deputy chief warned his lieutenants that if they ever openly criticized the administration he would yank them from their command. One lieutenant taped that diatribe and filed a complaint with the City's Labor Management Relations Board.

"He was trying to intimidate us," the lieutenant stated. "Others will not come forward because they are scared."

Back in 1994, in response to my question, "How is this going to end? " Betty Muench had told me:

"There is this group which is not understanding how things operate and they will be making their own rules. When this will border on anarchy, then they will fall, with truth coming out all around."

Was this the beginning of the fall? I certainly hoped so. My father had once remarked humorously, "Life is like a roll of toilet paper—the closer you get to the end, the faster it goes." At the time, I had thought that was funny. It wasn't funny now. When I'd stood at Kait's gravesite and told her, "Mother is going to get your killers," I couldn't have imagined how long that would take. Now I was feeling threatened by my own mortality.

The mayor told reporters, "When you have a department where there are accusations, counter-accusations, lieutenants accusing captains, captains accusing deputy chiefs, that is a department in disarray."

In the wake of that statement, the police chief resigned. He was given a hero's send-off by the police union, who threw a huge retirement party in his honor.

Experts were imported from California to analyze the evidence room problems. One of their suggestions was "Stop storing so much stuff!" Although valuable items were missing, (one woman had already filed a law suit claiming police had "misplaced" $100,000 worth of her family jewelry), there were over one million pieces of evidence crammed into the APD storage area.

The evidence room manager began to dispose of the items by selling them on E-Bay. The threat of a major purge threw us into a panic about the items from Kait's desk. Her personal property, including her telephone book, snapshots, and correspondence, might easily be considered disposable after fifteen years. Don submitted yet another request for their return, citing our concern for their safety. The new District Attorney agreed that we could have them. The Vietnamese correspondence was missing from the materials, but we now had pictures of some of Dung's friends in California. Not that they had any value, since the statute of limitations on the car wreck insurance fraud had long since run out.

The evidence room circus continued to provide entertainment for the nation. According to one article, three months earlier, a freezer in the evidence room that contained more than 1,600 samples of blood, urine, saliva and other evidence from rapes and homicides had been shut down. It was hardworking Sergeant Orr, who, although off duty that day, responded to a security alarm in the evidence room to find a door standing open. When she checked out the rest of the building she detected a foul stench and discovered the freezer had a temperature of sixty-eight degrees. The police and prosecutors had withheld that information from defense attorneys, who continued to construct their cases on contaminated evidence.

Although DNA evidence wasn't a factor in Kait's case, it was crucial to some of the other cases on our website. We hoped that those cases were not among the ones affected, because many of our Real Crimes families were depressed enough already. Several, who had been optimistic about breakthroughs, had been crushed to discover their cases could not be prosecuted.

Update—Nancy Grice's daughter, Melanie McCracken:
A grand jury indicted Melanie's husband, now-retired State Police Lieutenant Mark McCracken, on charges of first-degree murder and tampering with evidence. But the charges were dismissed on a technicality—an investigator for the prosecution was in the room during testimony.

Update—Bill Houston's daughter, Stephanie Houston:
The boyfriend who ran Stephanie over with his truck was brought to trial, but a jury found him not guilty of vehicular homicide. Police had not interviewed witnesses at the time of the incident, and, now that the case was four years old, the prosecutor would not call them.

Update—Arry Frank's sister, Stephane Murphey:
A judge declared the key jailhouse statement that incriminated David Bologh inadmissible because police had neglected to have him sign a waiver of his rights before taking his statement.
The district attorney said he would appeal the judge's ruling.
"We hear the appeal may take two or three years," said Stephane's mother, who had driven 1,000 miles from out of state to attend a trial that did not take place. "It feels like we're being tortured. We're being twisted slowly over a fire."

On Mother's Day, 2005, I experienced one of those dreams that left me feeling that I had received a message. It was the first such dream I'd had in over five years. But this time it wasn't Kait who delivered the message. The visitor who appeared at my bedside was the last person I would have expected, even in a dream.

It was Miguel Garcia.

Although I never had seen him in person, I immediately recognized him from newspaper photos. In the dream he was not in his thirties, as he would have been now, but was still the pimply-faced kid he had been when Kait was murdered.

Miguel handed me a Mother's Day card with a picture of the Virgin Mary on the front. When I opened the card, the message read, "I DIDN'T DO IT."

I looked up at the boy, who was standing there, waiting expectantly.

"If you didn't, who did?" I asked him.

Miguel said, "Juve." He paused and then added a bit nervously, "She told me to give you a hug because it's Mother's Day."

I didn't know if he was referring to the Holy Mother or to Kait, but either one was acceptable. In my dream state, I got out of bed and let him hug me. He was a strong but skinny kid, not much taller than I was, and it felt like being hugged by my teenage grandson.

Then Miguel's image disappeared, and I was awake.

I got out of bed, went into my home office, and recorded the dream. I had no idea what the source was—"Mary, Mother of Heartbreak"; Kait, reaching out to me on Mother's Day; or Miguel himself, asleep in Albuquerque, dreaming with such ferocity that his dream crossed the miles between us and merged with my own. I decided I would treat this information as I would any other tip. I would consider it a possibility until it was disproved.

Juve Escobedo? The man was an enigma.

APD's preferential treatment of Juve had always seemed strange. Although the men were arrested at the same time, police had held only Miguel. Even after both were indicted and a bench warrant was issued for Juve, police had not picked him up.

Over and over, psychics had described a shooter who sounded like Juve. Robert Petro had said, *"He has a very unusual first name, like a nickname. He appears to be around five feet eight, about 175 pounds, he has a police record, and he has somewhat dark skin, and he has what look like tattoos."*

Shelly Peck had been even more explicit: *"I'm getting a short name that starts with J. John? Joseph? And a Michael is involved somehow. And there's an S name. Or—'ES'—something? Was this person a mechanic? I get him disassembling cars. I get a vision of gas tanks, which is the symbol for a garage. Does he work in a garage, taking cars apart?"*

There was no way I could have influenced Shelly to make such statements. At the time of her reading I had not known about the body shop.

If Juve was connected to that, he quite possibly had disassembled cars. And Betty Muench had definitely placed him at that shop. *"The Hispanic suspect, Juve Escobedo, was there,"* she had written during one of her trance readings. *"This was after the death of Kait. He enters midst much attention and a sense of expectancy. He is to receive something."*

So how did my current Dream Visitor fit into the picture?

According to Betty, *"Garcia sought this so called 'honor' and must now undergo the pressure."* Was it possible that Miguel had accepted the assignment and hired the others as accomplices? In one of his drunken confessions, Marty had told police that he was paid one hundred dollars.

I went to the computer and pulled up information about Miguel. In February 1989, a warrant had been issued for his arrest for "aggravated assault." When I looked up the definition of that charge, it was, "An unlawful attack by one person upon another which results in severe or aggravated bodily injury and/or is accompanied by the use of a weapon or by means likely to produce death or great bodily harm." That was a very strong charge. What had Miguel done? I went back to the database to read the report by the officer who had gone to his home to arrest him.

It said a complaint had been made that Miguel had thrown an unknown object at a truck.

That came nowhere near meeting the criterion for "aggravated assault." However, the accusation of a felony, even if unfounded, had made it possible for that officer to obtain a warrant that allowed him to enter Miguel's home. Surprisingly, though, the officer hadn't arrested him. They'd apparently just had a chat and the cop had left. In his report he had listed an incorrect house number so people who read the report wouldn't know where Miguel lived.

Who was the cop who misrepresented the offense and then magnanimously let the fish off the hook?

I caught my breath as I realized why the name was so familiar.

He was the brother of Paul Apodaca's drug dealer, Lee.

The implications of such a situation were overwhelming. Roy Nolan had told Pat and me that narcs kept a stable of snitches who accepted assignments in exchange for money and protection. Miguel was in debt to this officer for not arresting him for "aggravated assault." Four months later, might he have been called to ante up?

But, even if Miguel had agreed to terrorize Kait, that didn't mean that he killed her. When police raided his home, they had found only one live cartridge and a single action revolver loaded with blanks. Blanks suggested intimidation, not murder. No blanks had been found in Juve's arsenal. Might Juve have been privately commissioned to kill Kait, while Miguel and Marty thought they were just going to scare her?

Neither Juve's Camaro nor Paul Apodaca's VW was a large enough vehicle to ram Kait's car with such force that it traveled over 700 feet, jumped the median, and ended up on the opposite sidewalk. But a police car could easily have done that. If a renegade cop had forced Kait off the road and fired a shot at her car to scare her, it was not impossible that Juve might have become excited, leapt from his Camaro and impulsively finished her off with a smaller caliber weapon.

In 1990, when psychic detective Noreen Renier had channeled Kait, she had described a scene that resembled the one I now was visualizing. *"I leave my friend's house and I'm cut off . . . They're coming to both sides of the car . . . I'm shot. Execution style."*

"I'm thinking along those same lines," Pat said when we compared theories. "I've suggested to the Cold Case detective that the Hispanics may have been hired to frighten Kait into keeping her mouth shut or to create a drive-by scenario to obscure a hit by somebody else. [11] He seems to find that concept interesting. He's going to interview Paul Apodaca in prison and try to find out what really happened at the crime scene."

"What about the resurfaced witness?" I asked her.

"I don't think he's made much progress with her," Pat said. "If he

189

discovers he's been fed a false lead, he'll go ballistic. This isn't a man who'll take kindly to being manipulated."

By now the Attorney General's Office had completed its investigation of the evidence room problems and announced that no one would be prosecuted. The two principal embezzlement suspects were reassigned to a different department. The manager of the evidence room, who was cited in an independent review as the person most responsible for concealing the thefts, resigned. She, then, was placed in charge of the New Mexico State Crime Lab. "We have no reason to suspect that she is anything but the best," said the spokesman for the Department of Public Safety. "We are quite fortunate to get her here."

The mayor expressed his pleasure that no uniformed officers were arrested.

The police chief was awarded his full retirement pension. He told reporters that he was looking forward to sleeping in, drinking coffee with artificial sweetener and cream, and watching football on television.

The only people to suffer were the whistle blowers.

I asked Pat when the Cold Case detective was going to interview Paul Apodaca.

"I don't know," Pat said. "It's been over a month since I've heard from him. I'll give him a call right now and ask him about that."

A few minutes later she called back, sounding stunned and disheartened.

"He's been transferred out of the Cold Case Unit," she told me.

CHAPTER EIGHTEEN

To: Lois Duncan:
Subject: Re: i worked w/kait at the import store
Wow, lo these many years later, and I hadn't thought about the whole tragic thing since I moved from Albuquerque shortly after Kait's murder! What a shock to stumble upon a website and all of the crazy goings on possibly connected! I used to work at that store when Kait was clothing manager, and I had a weird experience of my own. I found a packet of heroin in a box of fans. That was shortly before Kait was killed. I now live in a different state, but I've never forgotten Kait, even though she and I didn't know one another well. I have a child of my own, and can't imagine what you've gone through. Here's my phone number if you want to reach me. Sincerely,

Kim*

After all this time, the final pieces of the terrible puzzle were seemingly tumbling into place—the smuggling of drugs from the Orient; potential Asian recipients in place in Albuquerque; VIP drug addicts and/or administrators of drug cartels with easy access to drugs coming in from Mexico but no way to obtain the valuable white heroin from Asia; a crooked body shop where drugs were distributed—and Kait, planted solidly in the middle of all of those.

I phoned Kim. My heart was in my throat. What if she turned

out to be yet another fraudulent informant? What if she'd never worked at that shop at all?

But the moment I heard her voice—kind and concerned and intelligent—I sensed that whatever she had to tell me would be true.

"In 1989, my boyfriend and I were working as musicians," Kim said. "We traveled around a lot and stayed in various cities for short lengths of time. Every place we went, I'd get a day job to supplement what we earned in nightclubs. We were in Albuquerque nine months and I worked at that import store for two or three of those. I remember Kait being clothing manager but didn't know her well."

"What were your duties?" I asked her.

"I worked the floor and helped stock shelves," Kim said. "Shipments came from a central distribution center out of state. Boxes were stored in a back room, brought out one at a time as needed, and unpacked by whoever was available.

"When I found the heroin, it was evening and we were just getting ready to close. I unpacked a box of fans and discovered the packet. I recognized it as heroin because I worked in bars and was familiar with drugs. I also knew how the little packets were folded."

"Did you report it to the manager?" I asked.

"No, I didn't tell anybody who worked there because I didn't know who might be involved. Somebody there must have been expected to intercept it, but somehow missed it. Since it was only one packet, I'm guessing it was a sample and the game was just getting started. The major deliveries were probably scheduled for later."

Kim said she took the packet home with her. Then she phoned her brother, an out-of-state police officer, to ask him what to do. He advised her to call the FBI. Federal agents came to her apartment and seized the heroin. She never heard from them again.

A week later, Lenore*, the manager of the import store, was fired, allegedly because upper management paid a surprise visit and found the store "not up to merchandising standards." That came as a shock to everyone, especially Lenore. Kim said she went into work that day and found Lenore crying. She said Lenore was young and ambitious and prided herself on running a tight ship. She was a strict but fair boss, and all her employees respected her.

"She didn't deserve to be fired," Kim said. "She was doing a fine job. I've wondered if the feds might have contacted the home office and demanded to know what was going on at their Albuquerque store. They could have used a pretext to get rid of Lenore so they could bring in somebody from upper management to keep an eye on things."

Kait and Dung, horsing around. *(Credit: Kaitlyn Arquette)*

Dung in the import store where Kait worked. *(Author's collection)*

There was tension in the air, and Kim had started to get nervous. She quit her job and started working at a restaurant. Soon after that, she read in the paper that Kait had been shot.

"I was stunned," Kim said. "I'd never known anyone who was murdered. And the coincidence of the timing—Kait gets promoted to clothing manager; I find the heroin and turn it in; Lenore gets fired for some bogus reason; and a couple of weeks later Kait gets killed. All within such a short period of time."

"The stumbling block for me is the apparent randomness of the drug importation," I said. "The person who stuck that packet in with the fans must have intended it to go to a particular person. But if all the employees were arbitrarily unpacking boxes, how could they make sure the right person would intercept it? Especially if there were dozens of boxes, all coming in from the same distribution center."

"All of them were supposed to be from that distribution center," Kim said. "But that doesn't mean they all *were*. Many of the boxes came by UPS. The average employee, seeing those boxes come in, would assume they came from the distribution center, but they could just as well have come from a foreign country. If someone was alerted to watch for those particular boxes, they could intercept them on the loading dock or in the storeroom. Kait's boyfriend and his friends were in and out of that store all the time, visiting Kait."

Kim talked with Pat and reiterated all that she'd told me. She also agreed to put Pat in touch with her brother, who could confirm that Kim had told him about finding the heroin.

"Kim speculates that the new manager may have been assigned to check out the situation," Pat said. "That store wasn't computerized back in 1989. Since Kait was handling the invoices, he may have asked her to watch for incoming shipments that didn't match up with statements from the warehouse. If Kait told Dung about that, and he repeated it to people in the smuggling ring, that could have gotten her killed. That would account for his saying, 'This is all my fault!'"

"There's another possibility," I said. "What if Kait was ordered to intercept the heroin and refused to? Remember what Susan told her girlfriend about Kait's telling Dung, 'I know what you guys are up to, and I don't want to get involved.' That was only days before the murder."

"I want to know how Susan fits into this," Pat said. "How did she know about Kait's ultimatum to Dung? It's not likely Kait would have told her. But if, for some reason, she did, why didn't Susan report it after the shooting? She had plenty of opportunity."

"Are you suggesting that Susan may have learned that from Dung?"

"I don't know what part she may have played in this, if any, but she's told lie after lie, and there has to be a reason. When Susan applied to rent the space in front of that import store, she told the property manager she was doing so with an inheritance from her parents in Texas. I've run a background check, and her parents are alive and living in New Mexico. As soon as Kait died, she abandoned her cracked ice business, applied for Kait's job at the import store, and talked the new manager into hiring her boyfriend to work on the loading dock. Ten days later, they both stopped coming to work, without even picking up their paychecks. What does that add up to?" [12]

"It seems to suggest something I don't want to believe," I told her.

The state of New Mexico was in turmoil. Good and bad were tumbling like dominoes. When I pulled up on-line editions of Albuquerque papers, I was never prepared for what I might find:

State Treasurer Robert Vigil and former State Treasurer Michael Montoya are arrested on federal extortion charges. Montoya plea bargains and testifies against Vigil. Vigil is convicted and sentenced to prison. Montoya is later sentenced to prison as well.

Jay Rowland, Albuquerque's independent police review officer, is notified that his contract will not be renewed. Rowland states his belief that his ouster was orchestrated by the Police Union.

David Iglesias, U.S. Attorney from New Mexico, who publicly expressed his shock at the names of the VIPs in the buried narcotics report, is fired.

Manny Aragon, President Pro Tem of the New Mexico State Senate at the time of Kait's murder, is charged with fourteen counts of conspiracy, mail fraud and money laundering.

Ken Schultz, mayor of Albuquerque at the time of Kait's murder, is charged with similar offenses. He plea bargains and agrees to testify against Aragon.

Raul Parra, a contractor involved with the scheme, admits to skimming $3.3 million from the Metro Court audiovisual contract. Parra says he transferred more than $600,000 of the ill-gotten money to Manny Aragon. An outraged Aragon insists, "I am completely innocent!"

Toby Martinez, former Metropolitan Court administrator, is charged with similar offenses. He plea bargains and agrees to testify against Aragon.

When Manny Aragon realizes that the computer records and spreadsheets will now be allowed into evidence, he changes his plea to "guilty." The plea deal results in a sentence of sixty-seven months in federal prison (as compared to the eighteen years he would have received if convicted on all counts at a trial) and nearly two million dollars in fines and restitution. He is given a private send-off party by many of Albuquerque's most prominent citizens.

Manny's brother, Charles Aragon, pleads guilty to possession with intent to distribute almost half a million dollars worth of marijuana. He has two prior federal drug convictions, one for being chief finan-

cier of an international drug smuggling operation at the time of Kait's murder.

A newspaper article by Mike Gallagher reveals that former senator Aragon has been on the radar of federal agencies for over twenty years and has a long record of business dealings and friendships with convicted felons. It also discloses that Aragon was a partner in a construction business with Jerry Padilla Sr., a three-time convicted heroin dealer. The year of Kait's murder, Padilla was sentenced to ninety-six months in federal prison.

That same Jerry Padilla and his family head Los Padillas, the most dangerous street gang in New Mexico, known for distribution of heroin and other drugs.

And so, we have come full circle and are back to the drug scene—crooked political figures consorting with the state's narcotics king pins.

One of Betty's readings said that, to solve Kait's case, an investigation must *"start from the top and trace information downward."* I had assumed that this reading referred to the top tier of the police force.

Now I was starting to wonder if I'd misunderstood it.

JUNE 2010—
A SURPRISE ANNOUNCEMENT:

The Supreme Court of New Mexico has found that the 1997 amendment which abolished the 15 year statute of limitations for all capital felonies and first degree violent felonies, applies to all crimes committed within the 15 year period BEFORE its effective date of July 1, 1997. The State will now be able to prosecute all capital felonies and first-degree violent felonies committed after July 1, 1982.

In other words, the police department was wrong in their assertion that further investigation of Kait's case would be wasted. In the event that her killers are arrested and indicted, they will be able to be prosecuted, since her murder took place in July 1989.

In November 2012, the U.S. Department of Justice (DOJ) launched a two-year investigation of alleged corruption and dysfunction within the Albuquerque Police Department. This resulted in a scathing report, outlining deeply rooted problems with APD's culture; weak internal investigation, and rogue units. On October 31, 2014, the DOJ presented the current mayor of Albuquerque with a 106 page, court enforceable consent decree specifying that the city overhaul its use of force policies, recruitment, training, and internal affairs procedures.

Among the issues addressed in this agreement are the disbandment of the Repeat Offenders Project (ROP) team, some members of which—including Matt Griffin, "the Ninja Bandit"—were responsible for chasing down and shooting Peter Klunck, and a revamping of the Special Weapons and Tactics (SWAT) team, which, according to multiple sources, has been allowed to act with impunity for years. It also includes provisions for a civilian review agency to ensure the integrity of Internal Affairs investigations. The reforms, which will cost the City millions of dollars per year to put into place, will be overseen by a federal monitor.

I cannot help but recall Betty Muench's prediction:

"There are certain beings who will seem to be working on their own, but who have the abilities of training from higher authorities and thus can know the manner in which to infiltrate certain groups that will have to be inspected from the inside out."

The U.S. Department of Justice has the power to do that.

Although Don and I have agreed that Kait's personal case is of minor importance compared to the Big Picture, we have not lost hope that eventually it will be solved. From dozens of unrelated sources, a gigantic amount of information has accumulated to produce a convincing scenario that I never could have imagined at the time I wrote *Who Killed My Daughter?*.

I am a writer by trade, and now I have set the rest of Kait's story on paper. This is the best I can do until others come forward—those who will either refute my scenario or validate it.

And I feel in the depths of my heart that they *will* come forward to correct my inaccuracies and fill in the gaps in the story. Because, like Don and me, those people are aging. Each time they look in the mirror—or color the roots of their hair, or detect a lump in the breast, or experience a pain in the chest—they become aware of their mortality.

It won't be terribly long before they have to face Kait. [13]

EPILOGUE

Psychic Betty Muench died April 10, 2010.

Betty had often told me about a dream she had of one day publishing readings she had done for clients, (though only, of course,

(Photo by Lois Duncan)

with their permission). Her hope was to open people's minds to the possibility that the five physical senses that most of us regard as the only keys to reality may, in truth, be just the edge of a greater reality. Betty was the first to admit that she, herself, didn't know the extent of that reality. She considered herself a tool in the hands of "Spirit," a vehicle through which mental energy could be channeled. She said, "I have no more wisdom than anyone else—just a receptive mind, two hands, and a typewriter."

Betty—this Appendix is dedicated to you

APPENDIX

The following readings by psychics Betty Muench and Robert Petro are keyed to footnotes within the text:

CHAPTER SEVEN

1. Betty Muench, 9/18/93: What can you tell us about the wound that prevented Susan from attending Kait's funeral?

This is something that will have been very impromptu and came so suddenly that Susan could not move away from this and she will have been intimidated. This injury will have been inflicted by something ornate and available, an impulse of the moment. Susan will be one who will think of herself as impervious and very strong, but this incident with the cut will have been very sad for her in that it broke her spirit. This was what the true intention was, to shake her beliefs around this situation with Kait. She has no desire to be dishonest, but she is in so far over her head that she will be creating certain danger for herself if she talks. She does not even now know the whole truth.

This situation around Kait and the manner in which it was handled by authorities and by those actually involved was such that there has been harm done to many others, and Susan is one of the victims. Something was done to her, and it will have traumatized her. This has the sense of the Vietnam influence to it, but Dung will have been seemingly outside of this. Others seem to have taken this in their control.

2. Betty Muench, 10/08/93:

What may we know about Rod? Does he have any knowledge that can be of help to us?

There's an image of an African tribal mask which is large and would seem to cover the whole body and yet this is laid down on its side as if it is not in use. Kait is shown with a look of humor on her face, and she will point this out in flowing motions much like a representative would at a product show. She does not speak but seems to be saying, "See, there is no longer the mask!" and that will mean the mask of Rod.

There will be information which he will share. There is a key, a small and seemingly insignificant key, that he will possess, and he does not quite know what it is—something that Kait will have said to him in seeming jest, and yet it will be a key.

3. Betty Muench, 6/22/93

Would a focus on Dung bring any results? How best to affect his energy and bring forth some sort of movement around him?

This truth has been elusive and will have to be "dug" up in a sense. It is necessary to find the location of certain parties and to have them watched, and they will make mistakes. They have not quit their old activities, they have enlarged them, and this makes the possibility of trapping them even more important. This is not to falsely entrap but to allow them to snare themselves by repeating certain actions.

There is one who will be very interested in certain activities, and this will have to do with the Immigration people who will be very frustrated at certain efforts, and there will come information which will show that there is in essence an invasion of this country. Lois has an interest in something which the Immigration people also have an interest in. To tie this case in with certain other activity will be necessary at this time. This twist will be most alarming to many.

CHAPTER EIGHT

4. Betty Muench, 9/12/94:

What may we know about Pat Caristo and the role she is to play in finding the truth about Kait's murder?

There will be the sign of a teardrop shape, and that will symbolize all the tears shed in this situation. There will be this which is seemingly confined, and there will not be any further spilling of tears on this matter. Pat will be one who can bring this all together. There is in Pat the ability to utilize the information at hand which will need a certain interpretation which can be had from this more academic approach, and she will bring in certain contacts which will prove beneficial and will form the completion of the tear drop.

She will have great ability to advocate for others in similar situations, and this will keep her thread attached. Hers is a destiny unto itself. Pat is not in this for any kind of aggrandizement, but for the concept of justice, which is her karmic purpose in this time. She will know that she will be able to make contacts in ways that others cannot, and she can get information in ways that others cannot, and thus her assistance will prove very helpful to bring about all the energy patterns necessary to bring around this total symbol of the teardrop, the completed and whole teardrop.

5. Robert Petro, 9/20/96:

What link do you see, if any, between the Vietnamese, the Hispanics, and certain cops?

I feel that right in the heart of Albuquerque there seems to be some sort of garage or warehouse where they are doing alterations on automobiles. I feel that it includes local people as far as fixing up these cars, and they are changing the cars to transport out of state. I also feel that they have altered documentation and paper work, that it all appears to be forgeries. I believe that if the FBI was pulled into this case they could track the behavior of body shops, car shops, through their money in the bank. I feel they can be traced and caught.

CHAPTER NINE:

6. Betty Muench, 6/18/96:

What is the true source of the seeming fear or resistance of APD to confront the Vietnamese issue in Kait's murder?

There is this sense of the Vietnamese energy pattern which will come out of one particular entity, and this one will seem to be then swirled into the energy of the police department and it becomes like a tornado. This will have to do with this one man, and it is someone who is middle aged and who would not be an actual part of this group that Kait was involved with. This one will be more as a community leader, and it is as if he acts as some kind of liaison for this Vietnamese community. He will seem to have influenced the police department not to open up this problem.

This is someone who is well-meaning and who will seem to have some control over the community, but he is not strong enough to control the young so-called-warriors. There is this which the police did not want to confront, as they did not have the knowledge, and they will have been easily convinced that this was not necessary. There was the line of least resistance which the police department took on this, and justice did not seem to enter into it.

7. Betty Muench, 1/2/96:

What may we know about the true involvement of Roy Nolan in this investigation?

There is this image of Lois's head. She will seem to be a puppet and the head will turn all the way around. This will suggest that there is manipulation by some other force and this would not be what Lois would want to happen.

This seeming manipulation as depicted in this image will be only that which some others will have tried to put into her energy pattern, and they will not have made it through. Roy Nolan will have entered into this as a means to his own ends, but he will have been manipulated himself, and he will then have pulled out. The degree of his sincerity and ability in all this is to be questioned and his pulling out under some kind of coercion will not be that important to this situation. Lois is as well off without this influence. Nolan was making things fit so that he could ingratiate himself. There is no sense of loss here, and the head of Lois will not continue to turn in this manipulation of her thoughts.

CHAPTER ELEVEN:

8. Betty Muench, 10/4/95:

What guidance can you give us about what our next steps should be in furthering this investigation and bringing it to a successful closure?

There must now be the right-side applicant thinking, and this will go with the academic and intellectual. Lois and Pat can use the *masculine forces* now to further their case. It will be for Lois and Pat to think in terms of allowing the male energy to come into play, not necessarily to contrive how this will be done, but to let those available male energy patterns make their own suggestions and not simply have them voicing the opinions of the feminine aspect. Certain things are ready to go. There will be the stirring of the pot again, and there will come reactions.

9. Robert Petro, 9/20/96:

What do you feel about the involvement of the Albuquerque Police Department in what appears to be an obstruction of the investigation of Kait's murder?

To some extent that's true. But I feel that this only involves a couple of people, that it does not involve the department in general. I feel by the time the investigation got into the hands of the police department it was already diluted and all the evidence wasn't given to those investigating the murder. Those who collected the evidence are the ones who hid the evidence. I feel that the Albuquerque Police Department is standing and fighting, and they are right, because the evidence was tampered with even before it got to the police department.

CHAPTER SIXTEEN:

10. Who was the VIP Kait saw involved in a drug transaction?

Betty Muench—1990: "The person Kait saw is a political figure who has the podium and is very coveting of his position. He is married. He has a fear of being exposed that borders on paranoia, and this will have been part of his fear upon the observation of him by Kait. He will not have had anything to do with the actions after that, but his followers will be involved."

Nancy Czetli—1992: "He's active in both local city politics and state level politics. I think he's been in the state legislature. He may be part of your court system. He has black hair, he's heavy set, and is getting a little jowly under his chin. I'd say he's in his fifties and has a very powerful voice. This man has been involved for quite some time in rather extensive import-export of drugs. He did not order Kait's killing, but his presence helped trigger it."

Robert Petro (channeling Kait)—1992: "The VIP was in local

government. I can't give you the exact position, but he was a married man, well-positioned in government. But he wasn't the only one in the place. It appeared that everybody around there was doing something with drugs. For some reason I recognized him."

CHAPTER SEVENTEEN:

11. Robert Petro, 9/20/96:

The Albuquerque police arrested three Hispanic males—Miguel, Juve, and Marty. They claim they're innocent. What is your feeling about them?

There's involvement. But also I feel that they have somehow been used as a scapegoat. I somehow see them connected, but then I *don't* see them connected. But do they know something? The answer is absolutely yes.

CHAPTER EIGHTEEN:

12. Betty Muench, 7/17/02:

What may we know about Susan in regard to her cracked ice business and her motive for placing that cart in front of the import store? Were activities at the import store linked in any way with the circumstances leading to Kait's murder?

When Susan rented this space in front of the import store there was one with her who was very aggressive and who was supposed to be a kind of adviser, but this one could not contain his brashness.

The positioning of the cart will have allowed Susan an insight into an operation that was not sanctioned by any owner, but which will have been under the control of someone who was under the control of the brash one. The import store was not suspect, but some of those employed there will have knowledge. This would be a good record to have access to, for there will be many names on such a list that would figure into this death of Kait. Kait thought she had some allies, but indeed they all bolted on her when she needed them the most.

13. Betty Muench, 2/3/98: *What is the key to the ending of this case?*

There is this image of a female who will have her mouth bound with a gag and it is as if she is chewing through this until her own flesh will seem to be bitten off. There is in this, however, success, and she will be freed of this gag and able to scream out.

This is not Lois but another who will not have been able to say anything until now. The view showing the flesh being eaten away will be symbolic of her own internal stress eating away at her because of her inability to come forward.

This one breaking the gag on herself will be the key to the ending of this long struggle in this case around Kait's death. There is an image of someone who is coming to the end of something in her own life, and she will then want to come forward and make things balance in this investigation. This will mean that a great change is taking place, which will be outside the hands of anyone but that one person. That person is not someone who has been able to put guilt and grief behind her.

There is in this one the key to the ending of this case, which will not be able to be completed in the expected way, as this person would not be able to come to court with this. There will be in that then for Lois only the understanding. The need to understand all this is strong in Lois and it is not so much the need for retribution. It will be the need to know what Kait will have been going thru and who will have dealt her this hand which was not played out.

This is a story that will end with a kind of sigh, not a whimper or a bang, but a sigh all around. As others will come to also understand, there will be this which will permit Lois to lead others into a state of peace in so far as their own quests will be concerned.

For Lois this will be an ending, a closure to this chapter of her life.

"No book equals this one for credibility, bleak truth and mind-chilling horror."
—ANN RULE, AUTHOR OF
Fatal Friends, Deadly Neighbors.

Read the extraordinary story of what came before. Like *One to the Wolves*, *Who Killed My Daughter?* is a stand-alone book, complete with astonishing details found nowhere else.

Other books by Lois Duncan include:

Who Killed My Daughter?

Stranger with My Face

Locked in Time

I Know What You Did Last Summer

Killing Mr. Griffin

The Third Eye

Down a Dark Hall

Don't Look Behind You

Daughters of Eve

Summer of Fear

Ransom

The Twisted Window

Gallows Hill

Written in the Stars

To learn more about Lois Duncan and her books, please visit
our website at: www.planetannrule.com

Lois Duncan is an award-winning author of over 50 books, ranging from children's books to poetry to nonfiction for adults, but is best known for her young adult suspense novels. Six of her novels have been made into movies—including box office hits, *Hotel for Dogs* and *I Know What You Did Last Summer*. Duncan's prestigious awards include The Young Readers Award in sixteen states and two foreign countries, and she was named the 2015 Grand Master of the Mystery Writers of America.

Duncan and her husband, Don Arquette, raised their five children in Albuquerque, New Mexico, and now devote much of their time to seeking justice for their youngest child, Kaitlyn, who was murdered in July 1989. To learn more about Duncan, visit her website: www.loisduncan.arquettes.com and www.planetannrule.com.